# rage

# rage

## The True Story of a Sibling Murder

Jerry Langton

John Wiley & Sons Canada, Ltd.

Library and Archives Canada Cataloguing in Publication Data

Langton, Jerry, 1965–

Rage : the true story of a sibling murder / Jerry Langton.

Includes index.

ISBN 978-0-470-15441-0

1. Madden, Johnathon. 2. Madden, Kevin. 3. Fratricide—Ontario—Toronto. 4. Murder—Ontario—Toronto. I. Title.

HV6535.C33T67 2008 364.152'309713541 C2008-900613-5

**Production Credits**
Cover design: Jason Vandenberg
Interior text design: Mike Chan
Typesetting: Thomson Digital
Cover photography: MedioImages
Printer: Printcrafters

John Wiley & Sons Canada, Ltd.
6045 Freemont Blvd.
Mississauga, Ontario
L5R 4J3



This book is printed with biodegradable vegetable-based inks on 55lb. Rolland Enviro Natural Offset, 100% post-consumer waste.

Printed in Canada

1 2 3 4 5 PC 12 11 10 09 08

*Like everything, for the wife and kiddies*

# contents


**Acknowledgments** ix
**Introduction** xi

**Chapter 1:** Teenage Romance, a Tape Recorder and a Brutal Murder 1

**Chapter 2:** A Stepson's Revenge 20

**Chapter 3:** The Truth about Goths: Why Kids Want to Be Vampires 31

**Chapter 4:** Kevin's a Very Troubled Boy 66

**Chapter 5:** Big Brother, "Vampire Boy" and Friend Go to Court 95

**Chapter 6:** The Truth about Pretty Girls 126

**Chapter 7:** Starting Over 135

**Chapter 8:** Big Enough to Know Better? 144

**Chapter 9:** Another Year Older 152

**Index** 169

# acknowledgments

I'm at the fortress-like Toronto Police Central Station at Bay and College when Detective Sergeant Terry Wark greets me and takes me upstairs. He was the lead investigator on the Johnathon Madden murder case, and looks every bit the part. Except for the modern-cut suit, Wark looks like he just walked out of a Clint Eastwood movie from the 1970s. He's a homicide cop from central casting with an inscrutable face seemingly made of granite.

Upstairs, he introduces me to Detective Sergeant Glenn Gray, another big player in this drama. Gray has a much more jovial look about him, but still doesn't look like someone you'd want to piss off. I'm a pretty big guy, but Wark towers over me. Gray is taller than him.

Wark apologizes that the Toronto homicide headquarters doesn't look like they do on TV. I point out that I was thinking exactly the opposite.

They take me to a nicely appointed conference room and make a little small talk. Gray jokes about how often his name is misspelled in the media and recalls some of the worst ones, including the time he was called "Gray Glenn" by a local paper. I ask them a few questions about the case and I can tell that they are relieved that I know what I'm talking about.

Wark brings up a point about the tape. The tape is a key element in the case. A group of girls secretly tape-recorded some boys telling them they were going to murder a family. When they called the police, it set the wheels in motion for the eventual arrest of the boys. Not surprisingly, it was a valuable piece of evidence that both prosecution and defense tried to use for themselves. I admitted that I had not heard the tape, but had only read transcripts.

Wark then played it. Much has been written about how chilling the tape is to hear, and it truly is. The boys casually talk about murder as though it is no big deal. And the girl, taping them without their knowledge, appears to egg them on. One boy boasts about the plan, as though murder is something he does for fun. Another talks about it ambitiously, as though it will be his one great achievement and the solution to all his problems. The third treats it as a mere matter of fact, an annoyance he simply has to put up with.

So I have to thank Wark and Gray, not just for letting me hear the tape, but for giving me hours of their time and speaking frankly and accurately about every element of the case and trials. They set me straight on more than a few things I thought I knew, and I'm always grateful for that.

And if there's anyone who should be thanked for the existence of this book, it's Joseph Brean. It was Brean who uncovered the mountains of online evidence the police and lawyers missed. It was he who risked a contempt of court charge and potential humiliation by writing about it. And it was he who caused the first trial to end in a mistrial, forcing a second one with a more accurate picture, not just of the evidence, but of the people involved. When I approached him to help me with this book, he went well beyond the bounds of professional courtesy and provided me with an extensive amount of data and background. Very few true-crime books have heroes in them; but you're it for this one, Joe. It's not often a journalist can change the course of history just by reporting the facts, but he did. And on his first murder trial, too.

I also have to thank all the other police officers, emergency workers and journalists—particularly Peter Small—who helped out. And my thanks also go to the parents, friends, neighbors and other people who selflessly gave their time to help give me a clearer look at this complicated drama.

And of course, I must thank Joanne Champagnie, Johnathon's mother, for her cooperation.

As usual, I thank the team at Wiley Canada for backing this book. And Leta Potter, just because she doesn't want to be mentioned.

And this book, like most things I do, never would have happened if not for the help, patience and encouragement provided by my wife and two sons.

# introduction

I was talking with my agent in New York when I told him about a story. It was about a happy-go-lucky 12-year-old boy. He was a pretty ordinary boy—not special in any way—but a good kid with a kind heart. The problem was that he had a 16-year-old brother who wasn't quite so nice.

The big brother had some real problems. He was overweight and funny-looking. He'd failed both the seventh and eighth grades. He had severe anger issues, which led him to be passed around from school to school because nobody knew what to do with him. He'd been in the mental health departments at area hospitals so often that the staffs there knew him by first name.

The big brother hated the little brother. He tortured him, physically and emotionally. His hatred was rooted in the fact that his parents clearly preferred the little brother. Well, his mother at least. His father had abandoned the family on Christmas Eve when the brothers were four and eight. He was soon replaced by another man, but that caused even more problems. The stepfather not only favored the younger brother, but he tried to instill a system of discipline the older brother couldn't cope with. As an added twist, the stepfather was black and the son, white, an avowed racist.

The bigger brother brought a few other problems to the mix. He dabbled in Nazism Satanism, and vampirism. One day, he skips off school and invites over his friends—one of them a self-professed vampire who claims to kill people and drink their blood. They call the vampire boy's girlfriend and tell her all about the plan they have to kill the big brother's family. She hangs up, asks them to call back and tapes the conversation.

Then the big brother and his friends drink wine, smoke cigarettes and ransack the house. They are looking for money and credit cards so they can finance a killing spree in which they will target crowded public places with guns and bombs. When the younger brother comes home from school, he becomes the target of fatal violence.

That, I tell my agent, is when things get weird.

He stops me there. Misunderstanding me and thinking I was pitching a novel, he tells me that it would never sell, it's just not believable. Brother-on-brother violence? It's been done—since Genesis. A Nazi with a black stepdad? Come on. Teenagers who claim to be vampires and want to kill everyone because they think life is unfair? A little too Columbine, don't you think?

When I tell him that it all really happened in Toronto, he's surprised. "Truth is stranger than fiction, eh?" he says to me.

It really is. And, when I investigated the story that would later become *Rage*, I found that it was much stranger still. There are so many elements in the story, the murder of Johnathon Madden, that it would be hard to believe—a bit too pat to be true—if it were presented as a novel. In pursuit of the strange and the true, I take the reader along with me to some of the more extraordinary—and bizarre—interviews.

The victim really was an innocent young lad, who was remembered, more than anything, for being kind and thoughtful. The perps were lonely, nerdy, hateful boys attracted (in varying degrees) to racism, Satan and vampires. One of them—in a highly unlikely *Romeo and Juliet* scenario—became romantically entangled with a wealthy, talented, successful and beautiful young girl.

While the murder, arrests and investigation were almost pedestrian, the trials weren't. The first trial involved a tape recording of the boys detailing a plan not only to kill Johnathon, but his family and as many of the public as possible. It seemed like an open-and-shut case, until one of the prize witnesses was caught delivering compromising testimony.

My agent, as usual, is right. If this story was something I made up, I'd be embarrassed at how obvious it all is, how blatantly dramatic it is, and how well it all fits together. If I made it up, I'd be a total hack.

But, of course, I didn't.

Johnathon, as innocent as he was, did die. He was hacked to pieces by his older brother. And what happened before and after was a veritable soap opera of the obvious, the cliché, and the hard-to-believe.

While that may make for an unbelievable novel, it can make for a fascinating true-crime story.

*NOTE: The names of many of the youth in the book are not their real names, as their identities are protected under the provisions of Canada's Youth Criminal Justice Act. For that reason, care has been taken not to include identifying information.*

CHAPTER 1

# teenage romance, a tape recorder and a brutal murder

It all began innocently enough. Two young high schoolers—a 14-year-old girl and a boy who'd just turned 15—were on a first date at Toronto's Kew Beach in the autumn of 2003. They walked along the boardwalk, talking in the moonlight and listening to the lapping of the waves. It was the most romantic thing Tim Ferriman could think of on his very limited budget.

And it was also something of a re-creation of their first meeting. A week or so earlier, the two of them first saw each other when two groups of kids met up on the same boardwalk.

The two groups went to different high schools and came from somewhat different worlds. But they mixed and mingled, talking about this and that and laughing frequently.

Tim was shy, even among the kids from his own school. But something about him somehow caught the attention of the most attractive girl there. They started talking and, much to his surprise, she agreed to go out with him.

The date ended on one of those huge concrete blocks that jut out into Lake Ontario, that give visitors a chance to watch the waves and maybe throw a few stones into the water. They talked and talked until it got dark. At the end of the date, he got what he was after—she promised to see him again.

They made a strange pair. Ashley (not her real name) was pretty, verging on beautiful. Tim could tell a couple of things about her from what she wore: She had money and she was into a few things many of the other kids weren't. Ashley was not decked out in full Goth regalia, but there were subtle clues—her makeup, her jewelry—that indicated an interest in the occult. Tall and physically advanced for her age, she was often mistaken for a much older girl. She had thick dark hair, almond-shaped eyes and a long, almost regal, nose. In addition to her physical traits, Ashley was smart, personable and had a healthy sense of humor. A talented drama student at the prestigious Rosedale Heights School of the Arts, she was also an accomplished amateur photographer. She lived in one of the most desirable neighborhoods in the city, was well traveled and was surrounded by a well-to-do family dedicated to her cultural enrichment and her protection.

But because she was so very attractive at such a young age, she spent much of her time fending off the advances of prospective suitors. Her parents would not allow her to date at such a young age, but she decided it was time and defied them. She'd actually been dating regularly for about a year, switching from boy to boy without feeling much attachment to any of them.

Her choice of Tim was surprising, almost perplexing. He was not a particularly good-looking boy. He had the kind of face you could see a million times a day and never look twice at. He had small eyes, thin lips and a round, almost childish face. But he wasn't cute like a child, just plain. One girl I spoke with who remembered him from high school wondered aloud what Ashley saw in him, saying rather coldly: "No face, no body, no reason." Ashley's friends unanimously derided him as a loser.

Nor did Ashley (by her own admission) find him particularly intelligent, witty, well spoken or charismatic. He tended to wear the same clothes—almost always black—all the time and had few, if any, real friends. He lived above a second-rate sandwich shop with his dad in a run-down area of town. His mom had left when he was two years old after she decided that she'd rather feed her drug habit than her child. His dad's only source of income was a series of monthly disability checks from the government, and Tim had no identifiable income at all.

Part of what may have attracted her were the visual cues he displayed that indicated he wasn't just another jock, stoner or boy next door. Like Ashley, Tim didn't dress up in what has become the instantly identifiable Goth uniform. He was, instead, more subtle—although probably without realizing it. Tim showed his interest in things Goth with his jacket, his choice of T-shirts and his modest jewelry.

Tim was headed for a life on a downhill treadmill at a tough middle school until a guidance counselor intervened on his behalf and suggested he apply to one of the city's better high schools.

Although neither his marks nor his personality indicated that he deserved a better school, he was accepted by one and given an opportunity to escape the trajectory he'd been on.

But while he was accepted *by* the school, he wasn't entirely accepted *at* the school. A chronic truant with poor marks, frequently in trouble, Tim was also very unpopular at his new school. Most of his classmates I spoke with considered him something of a weirdo. None of his peers could name a single close friend of his at his new school.

Without an established social circle, Tim relied heavily on his old friends from middle school. But that all changed when he started seeing Ashley. She became his whole world. He saw nobody else, he spoke with nobody else and he thought about nobody else.

She wasn't as sold on their relationship as he was. They saw each other after school and in the evenings and kept in touch via e-mail and MSN Messenger—a popular real-time chatting application—every night for about a week or so. But while she was his only MSN contact, she had many. In fact, she maintained her enviable standing in all of her existing social circles. That included speaking with and flirting with other boys (which, of course, enraged Tim) and she spent a lot of time at home socializing through e-mail and on a number of different social networking websites. Tim—more cunning than intelligent—could sense that he was losing what little grip he had on her.

He was right. On one of their walk-around-the-neighborhood dates, she tried to gently break it off with him. She wasn't successful. After she broke the news to him, he panicked. He began crying and screaming about how much he loved her. Then he started breaking things—street signs, lawn ornaments—and smashing his fist into a wall. Unsure of what to do, she partially retracted her comments. She didn't exactly give him a vote of confidence, but she did somewhat ambiguously take back the dumping.

Although Tim did his best to deny the fact Ashley wasn't actually interested in him anymore, he knew she was on the verge of actually leaving him, so he decided to bring out what he thought was his only trump card. While their backgrounds were disparate, they had a few things in common—one thing in particular. Both of them had an interest in what he called "the dark side." Tim and Ashley talked for hours, fascinating each other with intense discussions about death-metal and Goth music, horror movies and the occult. Sensing that this was his quickest way back to her heart, he tried to appeal to her own dark side—something he later maintained had worked for him with girls in the past.

As their relationship waned, he convinced her to cut class one afternoon and took her to a coffee shop not far from her school. That's when he broke his big news to her—he told her he was a vampire. He could tell she was interested, but not really all that impressed. He told her that he liked to cut himself and drink his own blood. When she still didn't react enough, he added "before sex."

When that didn't get the reaction he wanted either, he looked around to see if anyone else was listening and began to tell her that he also drank other people's blood. He told her that he hid in the trees of the Don Valley—a ravine near where they both lived—ambushed unsuspecting joggers, killed them and drank their blood. It was a desperate ploy, and she seemed to recognize it as such.

A few days later, on Friday, November 21, 2003, Ashley called Tim at home to tell him it was over. Again, she tried to break it to him easy, to spare his feelings. She knew he was really into her and correctly surmised he was a very fragile person. But she knew she had to end their relationship to get on with her own life. She didn't want to be saddled with this guy any longer. He was just too immature and way too needy for her.

When Ashley dropped the bomb, he totally freaked out. Tim made a loud, strange noise, then burst into tears. Weeping, he told her that he loved her; he loved her more than anything. "How can you do this?" he asked. He was screaming and babbling, which made her even more sure her decision was an astute one. He said a lot of things, much of which she didn't understand because he was so frantic. So in an effort to calm him down, she let slip: "Forget it, never mind."

Tim was deluded enough to interpret the brush-off as a reprieve, so he called her again on Monday morning. After a great deal of pleading, she said she would allow him to visit her at her home the next day. She said she wasn't feeling well and was planning on calling in to school sick in the morning. But when he got in touch with her via MSN Messenger that morning, she told him he couldn't come over because her family had workmen in, renovating the house and she would get in trouble if her parents found out he had come around.

Distraught, Tim cut class anyway. He did little but feel sorry for himself until noon, when he decided to call an old friend from his old school.

Betrayed and humiliated by the gorgeous girl at the rich kids' school, Tim turned to her exact opposite. Widely regarded as the most bad-ass kid at Tim's old middle school, Kevin Madden was the antithesis of all things Rosedale Heights.

At a little more than six feet tall and about 250 pounds, 16-year-old Kevin dwarfed almost all of his classmates and teachers. While Tim was astoundingly plain, Kevin was just plain ugly. He had tiny, darting eyes sunk deep in his fleshy face with no discernible eyelids. His chin was severely undersized, making it look like his flabby neck ended at his lower lip. He had a thick, rubbery mouth and the kind of slow-working tongue that would make him sound stupid even if he wasn't.

Severe discipline problems had led him to attend 10 different schools despite never having moved. Whenever he got into major trouble, he was usually punished by being kicked out of school. Since it's against the law for someone his age not to attend school, he was always accepted by another, often less impressive school.

A classmate at the last of Kevin's schools, admittedly frightened of him, said to me that Kevin told him he wound up in that school because he had beaten up the principal at his last school. While that claim is almost certainly not true, it was widely believed and helped establish Kevin's reputation as a hardcore tough guy at his new school. And his size and quick temper gave him instant credibility.

Kevin was delighted to hear from his old friend. He told Tim that he and Pierre (not his real name) were cutting class and were "partying" at his house. Tim knew Kevin wasn't allowed to have guests over at his house, but he also knew both of Kevin's parents worked during the day, so he thought nothing of it. Tim accepted the invitation and hopped on the subway. He took up two seats.

Before long, Tim arrived at Kevin's house at 90 Dawes Road in Toronto's east end. Like much of the city, spiraling housing prices had led to a slow but steady gentrification of the area, but there were still pockets where the original working-class population was intact. Among the teenagers I talked to at the schools Tim, Kevin and Ashley went to, it had a reputation as a tough, racially mixed neighborhood.

Kevin shared the small, gray semidetached house with his 12-year-old brother Johnathon, his mother Joanne, his stepfather Ralston Champagnie and another family member who can't be identified. It was a tight fit and tempers sometimes flared in this blended family.

Particularly, Kevin didn't always get along well with Ralston. "They had all the typical father-son problems—you know, he was a teenager," a neighbor who knew the family well told me. "It was worse because Ralston was a stepfather, [and] he tried to move in and put in all this hard discipline, and Kevin didn't react well to that at all."

Kevin and Johnathon's biological father had split up with their mother on a memorable Christmas Eve about a decade earlier, and Ralston had moved in about four years after that. "And I don't even know how well the two of them [Ralston and Joanne] got along—they didn't always seem to," the neighbor said. "I got the sense Kevin didn't like the way he treated her . . . those boys were very protective of their mother."

She wasn't the only one I spoke with who questioned Ralston's ability to keep his anger in check. A former co-worker of his warned me "not to mess around with him," but declined to elaborate further. Despite his stepfather's intimidating presence, Kevin had decided to defy him that day and cut class.

When Tim arrived at 90 Dawes sometime around 12:20, he found Kevin and Pierre upstairs in the dark cell of a bedroom that Kevin shared with Johnathon at the front of the house. They were smoking and playing a video game. Pierre noticed that they had taken the mattress off one of the beds and propped it up to block the room's only window. Kevin explained that he blocked the window when he didn't want his stepdad to see what he was doing. Ralston would occasionally drive past the house, Kevin said, to look through the front window and spy on him. They had also taken a television from another family member's room and put it beside the one that was already there so they could play two games at once.

Tim had run into Pierre a few times before, but they weren't exactly buddies. Pierre went to Rosedale Heights with Ashley, though they weren't friends. They knew each other by sight and by name—pretty well everybody in the school knew who Ashley was—but they didn't have much in common. Instead, Tim knew Pierre through Kevin. Pierre and Kevin had grown up in the same neighborhood and, although they had taken different academic paths, they remained pretty close. More than a few observers have characterized their relationship as one that featured Kevin as a fearsome and impulsive leader and Pierre as his submissive, admiring follower.

The boys had grown tired of the video game—*Deathtrap Dungeon*, a *Dungeons & Dragons* knockoff that one reviewer called a "typical hack and slash" game—and had moved downstairs to watch the big TV in the living room. Somehow, Kevin had gotten his hands on a hardcore porn DVD. He played *Eat My Pussy*, an oral sex–themed compilation film four hours long, but the boys soon lost interest.

Kevin suggested they drink some of Ralston's red wine. Tim knew that staying and drinking the wine was a pretty big step to take, one they couldn't back down from later on. Ralston would obviously see that the wine was missing, and it would be nearly impossible for them to replace it. Although 16-year-old Kevin was big, he was clearly underage; and both Tim and Pierre looked, if anything, younger than their 15 years. The prudent thing to do, he knew, would be to get out of the house before Ralston came home, and let Kevin deal with the aftermath. Tim didn't get wine very often and was always up for a good drunk.

Kevin got some wine glasses and filled them for himself and his friends.

Bored with the DVD, they abandoned the living room. Kevin got an idea. He told Pierre to go get his baseball bat from his room. Kevin wasn't really into sports, that was more his little brother's thing, but there were two bats—one wooden and one aluminum—in their room. Pierre gave Kevin the wooden one and kept the aluminum one for himself.

Because Ralston worked as a chef at Shopsy's—a popular downtown delicatessen famous for its hot dogs—and at the Air Canada Centre, he was familiar with handling large amounts of food. He liked to buy in bulk at big-box stores and always had a few one-gallon jars of mustard, ketchup or relish sitting around the house.

Kevin found a mustard jar and placed it on a coffee table in the basement. Pierre handed him the wooden bat and Kevin took a Ruthian swing at the jar. The glass exploded into a billion pieces and mustard flew everywhere, splattering Kevin, Pierre, Tim and most of the room. The boys hooted their approval as Kevin twirled the bat in triumph.

He felt like raising the stakes. The family had an old TV down the basement. It didn't have cable, but it was hooked up to an equally ancient VHS player. Kevin pulled the bat back and swung at the screen's dead center. When the bat hit, the reinforced glass screen shattered into a spider-web pattern with a dull thud. Apparently disappointed by the anticlimactic result, he kept smashing at it until it imploded and smoke started coming out of it.

Their caution suddenly erased, Pierre and Tim joined in. Emboldened, Kevin looked for something else to smash. In an instant, he found what he wanted to destroy. Ralston had a fondness for Heineken and usually had a cache of empties in the basement. The boys lined a number of the green bottles up on the table and Kevin smashed them one by one.

Bang! Followed by shouts of "awesome!" Then they lined up another set and, this time, Pierre swung as hard as he could. Pow! It felt very good for these very frustrated and down-on-their-luck young men to exercise their ids in this way. A few more whacks and they were through all the beer bottles. But that wasn't the end. Encouraged by their own destructive pursuits, the boys went on a small rampage.

Kevin told his friends that his parents kept money in the drawers of their dresser and the boys immediately raced to their bedroom. They emptied the drawers—throwing the contents on the bed and the floor—but didn't find much money. They did, however, manage to secure some identification and a couple of credit cards. Pierre also found a pair of handcuffs with neon pink fun fur on the bracelets. He twirled them on his index finger and laughed. It didn't make Kevin like Ralston any better.

With nothing left to smash, the boys started looking for something else to do. They took the meager amount of money they'd found in the upstairs bedroom and went to a nearby convenience store. Kevin picked the one he knew would sell him cigarettes. They bought smokes and chips and other junk food, then returned to 90 Dawes.

At 1:31, Tim talked them into calling Ashley. The other boys didn't want to. Kevin even labeled the idea of calling a girl "gay," without sensing any irony. But Tim persisted and eventually got his way. He told Kevin that Ashley was really into vampirism, which seemed to change his mind.

She answered. At first he was a bit abusive to her, asking her crudely sexual questions about her family. She wanted to hang up, but he kept her on the line with an enigmatic boast. "You're not going to believe this," he told her. "We're planning something big—you'll hear about it on the news." Intrigued, she asked what he was talking about. Finally feeling a little advantage in their relationship, he shouted: "None of your concern, bitch!"

Now she was really going to hang up. The only thing that stopped her was call waiting. She excused herself and accepted the other call. It was her dad, checking in on her. Ashley had told him she was under the weather, and he wanted to make sure she was taking care of herself. She assured him she was okay and got rid of him. She realized that Tim's calling her a "bitch" could be her out, it could be the excuse she needed to finally break it off with him.

When she got back to Tim, she heard him talking to some other boys. She couldn't make out what they were saying, but could tell they were excited. Her curiosity once again aroused, she asked him what he was talking about. He asked Kevin if it was okay to tell her. Kevin gave him his permission. Tim then detailed a plan in which he, Pierre and Kevin would kill Kevin's family, steal his parents' cash and credit cards, use the money to buy weapons and explosives and then bomb malls and highways, killing as many people as possible.

Ashley was stunned. While she didn't believe that Tim really killed joggers in the park to suck their blood, she was very concerned by the phone call. Tim was desperate to impress her and capable of just about anything. Ashley had never met Kevin, but she had heard a little about him and knew that he was something of a tough guy, one with little or no feeling for anyone other than himself. She quickly ran through her options. She didn't want her parents to know she was dating behind their back—especially a guy like Tim—so telling them was out. She didn't have much respect for them anyway. The cops were an even worse idea. Not only would they ask all kinds of embarrassing questions, but they'd probably end up telling her parents anyway. After all, she was only 14.

She decided instead to tell her oldest and most trusted friend Heather (not her real name). She dialed *69 on her phone, wrote down Kevin's number, got dressed and caught a bus for school.

While Ashley was on her way to school, Ralston got his first break at work. As a chef at Shopsy's—a restaurant especially popular with commuters and tourists—he was bogged down by the lunch rush until after 2 p.m. But he was very concerned about Kevin. They had had another big fight on the weekend, and Ralston had punished his stepson by revoking his privileges on the family computer. It was a crushing blow. Using the computer was Kevin's favorite pastime, and since he'd been banned from it, he'd grown more surly and standoffish than ever. Ralston was pretty sure he'd heard Kevin saying something about "skipping off" (cutting class) on the phone. Eager to find out if Kevin went to school or not, he called home at 2:13. The phone rang and rang, but there was no answer.

* * *

Ashley got to Rosedale Heights at 2:15 and caught Heather on her way out of drama class. Ashley was so obviously distraught that Heather immediately realized she had to calm her down before they could talk. A few friends who also saw how upset Ashley was and were eager to help gathered around as she told her dramatic tale.

The group decided that, even though Ashley would definitely face punishment from her parents, they had to go to the police to keep anyone from being murdered. In the end, her parents might even be proud of her if she saved lives. But Heather pointed out that the police might not believe the word of a 14-year-old girl. And, even if they did, it was just her word against his. And what if it was all just a big joke or an elaborate stunt to get Ashley interested in Tim again? He had lied to her about killing people before.

But what made the difference this time, Ashley told her friends, was that the murders were yet to happen and that Tim had identified the victims. If they didn't end up dead, Tim wouldn't be able to pretend he was a killer anymore. It just didn't make sense. And he wasn't alone; he was with Kevin, some tough guy from the vocational school that Ashley didn't know, and Pierre.

"*Pierre* Pierre?" one of the girls asked in disbelief. They all knew who he was—he went to Rosedale Heights and he was the only Pierre in the school—but none of them thought all that much of him. He was nice enough, but there was nothing special about him.

"There's a quick way to see if he's telling the truth about that," Heather said. "We'll find out if Pierre is here [at school today]." But there was a problem with her plan—none of them knew Pierre's last name. So Heather took Ashley to the library so they could look through a yearbook for him. After they found him, they headed to the office to page him. They hadn't thought of an excuse, but didn't really need one. As soon as they asked the school secretary if they could page him, she responded that Pierre hadn't come to school that day.

Pierre's absence added even more credibility to Tim's claims, and the girls regrouped to form a plan. But the problem remained that they had no evidence other than Ashley's word. And to make matters worse, she didn't know Kevin at all, not where he lived or even his last name. But she did, through her use of *69, have his phone number.

That's when one of the friends, Lindsay (not her real name) had an idea: Why not call the boys back, ask them about the plan and tape-record the whole thing. She had, she said, tape-recorded a few phone calls before—as a joke, of course—and still had the recorder at home. Heather asked her if they needed anything other than a tape recorder. Lindsay said she guessed not. So they decided to go to Heather's house—she had a nice new tape recorder, after all—after school and call the boys back.

One of the girls chickened out at that point, but two more were added, for a total of five.

* * *

While Kevin and his buddies were trashing the house and Ashley was waiting to talk to her friend, Johnathon was just anxious to get out of school. It wasn't that he didn't like school; he was just excited about getting out. The same wintry weather that depressed Tim and made Ashley sick delighted Johnathon. The sun had come out that afternoon and he knew that would make the snow that fell the night before turn into packing snow, perfect for a snowball fight.

The bell rang at 3:20 as usual, but his entire class was required to stay late due to a detention. It wasn't uncommon for this class to be held back if there was an infraction nobody owned up to (and nobody squealed) and they waited quietly for the time to pass. At 3:30, Johnathon grabbed his bag, shot out of class, ran across the street and grabbed a double handful of snow. Snowball fights are against school rules, so Johnathon and his friends instinctively found each other across the street and were quickly firing snowballs at each other's heads. They grabbed snow from the ground and scraped it off the hoods of parked cars. They were laughing and having a great time until Jeffrey's mother stuck her head out their front door and called him in. He was grounded and not allowed to play any more. The irony was that he was grounded for leaving school grounds at recess—he'd gone home, across the street, to get gloves to be ready for the snowball fight. Jeffrey begged his mom to let him stay in the fight, but she said no. He asked if he could "at least" go over to Johnathon's house. Normally, Jeffrey was allowed to go to his pal's house after school, but grounded is grounded, so she said no.

Johnathon didn't want his buddy to get in trouble, so he said goodbye to Jeffrey and looked for someone else to hang around with. He was in no hurry to get home.

After a while, he spotted Jamal (not his real name). Jamal was a few years younger than Johnathon, and Johnathon worried about him. He was a nice kid, but didn't have many friends and he had to walk home all by himself because his parents and older siblings never seemed to be around. Johnathon liked him and didn't like the idea of him crossing the busy Danforth all by himself, so he decided to walk him home, even though it was a few blocks out of his way.

* * *

Ashley and the girls raced to Heather's house. Heather's mom was already home and the girls blew by her on the way up to Heather's room. Her mom stopped them and asked what was going on. Heather wouldn't explain, but told her it was serious. Rather than pry further, she gave them their privacy. But she also assured them she'd be around just in case they needed her.

Sitting on Heather's bed, Ashley took Kevin's number out of her pocket and dialed. One of the girls noticed it was written down in pink highlighter. Lindsay held Heather's tiny tape recorder up to the phone receiver. It was 4:13 when Kevin answered the phone. Ashley asked for Tim. Kevin put him on. He tried to play it cool.

Tim: Hey, what's up?
Ashley: Not much, what are you guys up to?
Tim: Nothing. We're here waiting.
Ashley: Waiting for what?
Tim: What do you think?
Ashley: I don't know.
Tim: His family to come home.
Ashley: Why?
Tim: 'Cause we're going to kill them.
Ashley: Good job.

Later in the conversation, Ashley pressed Tim on his part in the conspiracy.

Ashley: Are you actually going to?
Tim: You thought we were joking?
Ashley: A little bit.
Tim: A little bit.
Ashley: Anyway.
Tim: Oh please, like you know I couldn't resist. (Laughs)
Ashley: (Laughs)
Tim: Killing somebody, Jesus!
Ashley: Anyway . . .
Tim: Should know me better.
Ashley: All right then.
Tim: I was just an accessory that came over and they're like, yeah, we're going to kill them. I'm like, well, I'm not really [going to] do a lot. More like sit there and drink blood, but okay, fine.
Ashley: Pierre's going to?
Tim: Yeah, Jesus Christ, [unintelligible]. Pierre's gonna kill a lot.
Ashley: Are you serious?
Tim: Yeah.

At this point, Tim asked Ashley what she was doing that night. She demurred and eventually said that she was thinking of doing something with him, but since he was busy she couldn't. He freaked out. Tim could hardly believe that Ashley wanted to see him again. He made it obvious that it he was dealing with a dilemma: He would have loved to be with her, but he had a prior commitment he couldn't get out of. Exasperated, he says: "The one time I can see her . . . Why do I have to kill someone *today*?"

That's when he got the idea that she could come to the house. He told her she could come over and watch. He did his best to sell the idea. "You'll just be an accessory," he offered plaintively. When she refused, he told her that the two of them could "hang out in the bedroom while" Kevin and Pierre murdered the family. She refused again. After she demurred repeatedly, he kept pressuring her to come over by cloyingly saying, "blood is on tap here," as though he was giving her a gift of human blood to drink.

Throughout the call, the other girls had been writing down suggested questions and showing them to Ashley. When one note instructed her to talk to the other boys, Ashley asked to talk to Pierre, who Tim had mentioned in the first call was with them and whom he was aware she knew from Rosedale Heights. The first thing she did was to make sure this Pierre was the shy, unimpressive Pierre they all suspected it was.

Ashley: *Pierre* Pierre?
Pierre: Yeah.
Ashley: So you're killing people now?
Pierre: Yeah.
Ashley: Since when?
Pierre: Since today.
Ashley: Really?
Pierre: Yeah.
Ashley: Good job.

Finished with him, she decided to move on to Kevin. She'd never met Kevin before, but asked for him anyway.

Ashley: How are you?
Kevin: I'm fine, you?
Ashley: Not bad. You having fun planning the deaths of your parents and little brother?
Kevin: Oh, it's already planned . . . it's already planned.
Ashley: Oh . . . I see, you're just waiting now?

Kevin: Pardon?
Ashley: What time are your parents and your brother getting home?
Kevin: You know, my brother should have been home by now—but for some fucked-up reason, he's not home yet.
Ashley: I see.
Kevin: It's like he knows what's happening . . . so he's avoiding it.
Ashley: Awwww . . . puppy. What time do your parents get home?
Kevin: Ah, my father's supposed to be home early today. My mom may be home around 8:30.
Ashley: Good job. So where are you doing it? Your basement?
Kevin: Doing it right here. Wherever they come in.
Ashley: Really?
Kevin: Yes.
Ashley: Good job. What do you guys have?
Kevin: Uh . . . fists and knives.
Ashley: Oh, no guns?
Kevin: I'm not using a gun—too loud.
Ashley: Ah.
Kevin: Too loud. Too easy.
Ashley: Uh, why are you doing it?
Kevin: I'm just sick of everything.

That's when Tim took the phone back from Kevin. Ashley later described him as sounding ecstatic at this point. She asked him why they were doing all this. Tim hesitated. Then he called out to Kevin: "What are your reasons again . . . other than that you hate your stepfather?" Although he was already across the room, the tape recorder caught his shouted reply: "I hate my parents . . . I hate motherfucking everything."

Tim started begging her to come over again. He offered her money. She refused. He eventually offered her drugs (which he didn't have)—but she continually refused. Eventually she went back to her original story of being sick, and she said that she was tired and wanted to go to bed. Reluctantly, he let her go.

As soon as she hung up, Ashley—the talented drama student—broke character and burst into tears. The other girls excitedly ran downstairs to tell Heather's mother about the call. They played her a portion of the tape and she told them she had to call the police right away. Ashley stayed upstairs, crying.

At 4:34, Constable Paul Wildeboer received a call from dispatch about a death threat. He and his partner arrived at Heather's house at 4:42 and were surprised by what they heard. The girls played them the tape, and both cops immediately recognized the gravity of the situation. The police took the girls' statements, the tape and Kevin's telephone number. They were disappointed they didn't get his address—because getting it would mean a trip back to the station and a network search—but they were very impressed by the girls' detective work, and they told them so. Wildeboer even compared Ashley to Nancy Drew. He then asked them what gave them the idea to tape the phone call. Lindsay told him it was because the police don't always believe what teenagers say.

* * *

Ralston didn't normally get out of work until much later, but on November 25, 2003, he finished up at Shopsy's just before 3:00 p.m. Working two jobs six days a week left him with very little time to himself, so he decided to enjoy what little time he had. On his way home, he stopped at the old Greenwood Raceway. The horses haven't run at Greenwood since 1994, but the housing development that now stands on the old racetrack grounds still has a betting parlor—a tip of the hat to the track's former glory. Ralston enjoyed just hanging around, betting on the horses (which now ran at the Woodbine track in the faraway western suburbs) and watching the results on the betting parlor's many TVs. He even had a few friends there. Ralston was having a great time until the clock caught his eye. It was 4:45 and he knew he'd better get moving. He wanted to get home by 5:30 to make dinner for the kids.

* * *

Sean, a good friend of Johnathon's, had been looking for him since 3:20. Actually, Sean—in a different grade—got out at 3:10, but habitually played basketball with some other school friends until his buddy's class got out. Despite their slight age difference, Sean and Johnathon were very close, often walking to and from school together, going to each other's houses and even on one another's family outings from time to time. But what they used to like best was to go down to the cyber café and play online video games together. Johnathon had developed a passion for video games, but rarely ever got to play them at home because Kevin dominated the family's computer. At the cyber café, he could play online games like *Runescape* for just a few bucks and have a good time with his friends while he was there. He'd gotten to know many of the cyber cafe's habitués and staff and really enjoyed himself while he was there, even when he wasn't actually playing.

On November 25, Sean—as usual—spent the time between 3:10 and 3:20 p.m. shooting hoops with a few other friends. When Johnathon didn't come out at 3:20, he decided to go home and watch TV. Sean quickly got bored and called Johnathon's house to see if he wanted to come to the cyber café. Kevin answered. Sean recognized his voice, but didn't really know him well enough to chat. He asked if Johnathon was home. Kevin told him he wasn't there and hung up. Fed up, Sean went to the cyber café by himself at 4:20.

Not only wasn't Johnathon there, but nobody else he knew was either. Disappointed, he plunked down a toonie and sat in front of a rented PC.

Sean was well into his game when Johnathon finally showed up. Since Sean was in the middle of a game, etiquette commanded that they not talk much. When Sean glanced at the clock, it was 4:40. Johnathon asked him if he could borrow some money to play. No way, Sean said. Not only had he spent his last toonie on the game he was playing, he was tired of bailing him out all the time.

Embarrassed, Johnathon chuckled and shrugged and said he was going back home to get some money. He had a roll of quarters in his room.

* * *

Wildeboer returned to the stationhouse at 5:05 to find an address for Kevin's telephone number. Since he was shocked by the content of the tape, Wildeboer handed the statements, tape and other evidence over to Detective Sergeant Glenn Gray of the Criminal Investigation Bureau. Gray remembers that Wildeboer said to him: "You've got to hear this tape, it's no run-of-the-mill death threat." But Gray didn't have time to listen to the tape yet. He accepted

Wildeboer's assessment of the situation and called Kevin's number to see if the boys were still in the house. When Kevin answered at 5:32, Gray pretended to be a telemarketer. "I wasn't trying to sell him anything, just taking a survey," Gray said later. "It was something annoying, something nobody would ever want to do—I just wanted to get him off the phone quickly." Kevin was calm and unfailingly polite. Gray quickly determined that Kevin was not only still at the house, but that his friends were still with him and his parents weren't home yet.

Gray told Wildeboer and his partner to go to 90 Dawes and arrest all three boys. "If the parents are home and give you any trouble, just get the three guys into custody, and we can play the tape for them," he said.

* * *

As soon as he got home, Johnathon ran upstairs to get the quarters from his room. He knew something was very wrong immediately. Kevin, Tim and Pierre were in there, drinking wine and smoking, and they had made a complete mess of the room. Johnathon looked at Kevin and said: "I'm telling mom and dad." Before anyone else could react, Kevin grabbed his little brother by the arm and dragged him down the stairs.

Downstairs, Kevin and Pierre began to threaten the 100-pound Johnathon. They told him that they'd totally trashed the basement and that he wasn't going to say anything to anyone because he wouldn't be able to.

Johnathon just sighed. He'd lived through his big brother's rages many times before. They both knew Kevin was much bigger, stronger and faster than him. Johnathon came up to his brother's sternum, and his chest was no bigger around than one of Kevin's thighs. There was nothing he could do. He couldn't get away. He couldn't fight back. Even if he managed to hurt his big brother, he knew instinctively that Kevin would never, ever give up. If he fought back—especially with Kevin's friends watching—it would only get worse for him. Johnathon realized he just had to put up with whatever Kevin was going to do to him, and he prayed it wouldn't be too embarrassing in front of the other boys.

Kevin said he was going to "kick his head in," which was popular slang among their group for beat up, and something Johnathon would not have taken literally. Pierre seemed to like the idea of beating up Johnathon, and he quickly hooted his approval. Only Tim demurred, openly asking: "What's the point?"

Sensing his chance, and attempting to defuse the situation, Johnathon asked to see what the boys had done downstairs.

As soon as Johnathon got to the top of the basement steps, Kevin slammed one of his outsized fists between his shoulder blades, knocking him down the stairs. Then he told Tim to go get a butcher knife from the kitchen. He did. Tim was very nervous by this point, and when he handed Kevin the butcher knife, he later claimed to have told him: "Just threaten him and get him out of here."

Whether Tim said that or not, Kevin had other plans. He ran down the stairs and got on top of his much smaller brother, who was just getting up from the basement floor. After pulling it up behind his head, Kevin plunged the long, thick butcher knife into Johnathon's face. Then he began pumping the knife back and forth, up and down for what seemed like hours, each time striking at his younger brother's face and neck. Tim could see Johnathon holding his hands in front of his face out of instinct and Kevin slashing them out of the way.

There was almost no screaming. Johnathon was just too shocked. Pierre—who had fled to the living room—and Tim were too stunned to make any noise. And after Johnathon's voice box was slashed and rendered useless, the only noise audible over the music was Kevin's repeated pounding of the knife into his brother and Johnathon's gurgling on his own blood and desperately gagging for breath.

After his brother drove the thick stainless-steel blade through his skin, muscle and bone so many times that Tim lost count, Johnathon was lying on the basement floor struggling for breath, bleeding out and dying.

CHAPTER 2

# a stepson's revenge

Ralston Champagnie was a big, strong man. Though not very tall, he carried a solid 250 pounds on his stout, powerful frame. He had thick arms, big hands and wide shoulders. What's more, he had eyes that seemed to convey a deep inner anger, a look that meant he was indeed not a guy to be messed with.

According to many sources, stepson Kevin Madden had messed with him a few times. The two simply didn't get along. Ralston was a strict old-school disciplinarian, and Kevin had a very hard time fitting into his idea of how a household should run. Although nobody said that they had ever seen Ralston physically abuse Kevin, every source I spoke with—even those who described themselves as the man's friends—acknowledged that Ralston rode him hard, often humiliating him in front of family and friends, and that Kevin bore him a profound and festering grudge. The pair had finally attended family counseling with Kevin's mother, Joanne, and had come to a workable solution: from that point forward, Kevin's discipline was to be Joanne's responsibility; if Ralston found Kevin doing anything wrong, he was supposed to report it to Joanne and let her sort it out.

At work on November 25, 2003, Ralston was nervous about Kevin. Things had been extra tense at home since he had taken away Kevin's computer privileges. He'd broken the agreement made about a month earlier, not to punish the boy, by barring him from the PC after a particularly galling display of insolence. Ralston later felt a need to extend the punishment when he caught Kevin on the computer after he was forbidden to use it. Kevin enjoyed his time on the family computer more than anything else and was deeply resentful that his stepfather had taken it away.

Ralston had overheard something about Kevin planning to skip school that day, and wanted to catch him in the act. He had phoned the house, but there was no answer. That could mean he was at school, or that he was smart enough not to pick up.

Ralston was angry and ready to deal with Kevin when he got home. But he wasn't ready for what he found.

He drove up the alley behind the house, parked his old minivan and walked up through the back yard. As he made his way through the back yard up to the house, he noticed Kevin, a defiant look on his face, standing at the back window staring out at him. Although Kevin rarely stood up to him and never in any meaningful way, Ralston knew he was in for something of a fight, so he steeled himself for a confrontation.

Ralston didn't have a key, so he motioned for Kevin to let him in. Kevin ignored him. Angry and confused, Ralston tapped on the glass and repeated the gesture. Kevin eventually complied, but when Ralston got to the door, Kevin blocked his way. Ralston was taken aback. He knew that Kevin had gotten big, but he had never been confronted with his strength before. Even so, Ralston—just as heavy, but about three inches shorter—pushed him aside.

Once inside the house, Ralston confronted his stepson. "You smell like smoke," he said. Kevin was not allowed to smoke, and he knew he'd get in trouble if he got caught, so, out of reflex, he made up an excuse about hanging around with some kids at school who were smoking. The smell, he claimed, must have come from them.

Ralston sat down in the living room and was unnerved to see Kevin looming over him, nervous and expectant. Ralston could see wine glasses with cigarette butts in them scattered around the room and smoke in the air. Suddenly, a boy he didn't recognize (Tim) came running down the stairs frantically. Kevin wasn't allowed to have guests without a parent present and not at all when he was grounded, and Ralston became very angry. "What are you doing in my upstairs?" he yelled at Tim, more for Kevin to hear than the younger boy. Tim and Ralston locked eyes, and the frightened teenager, tears welling in his eyes, cried out: "I'm sorry, I'm sorry," and fled through the front door.

At about the same time, a very sheepish-looking Pierre emerged from the basement. That cut it for Ralston. Not only had Kevin been smoking, but he had two guests over, one of which had clearly done something stupid. Instead of losing his temper entirely, he decided to call Joanne, Kevin's mom, who was at work. He told Kevin exactly what he was doing.

Kevin slapped the phone out of his hand, shouting, "No, you're not!"

That was enough; Ralston knew he had to put his foot down before things spiraled totally out of his control. "What are you doing?" he bellowed.

That's when Kevin lunged at his stepfather with the butcher knife—already severely chipped and scored after Kevin's attack on Johnathon—stabbing at his heart. As it happened, Ralston hadn't taken his winter coat off yet, and the knife got caught up in it, barely penetrating it to his skin, leaving a small but nasty scratch.

But Ralston didn't know that. The shock of the attack and the pain of the impact convinced him that the knife had entered his chest, endangering his life. Aware Kevin wouldn't turn back now that the stakes were life or death, Ralston leapt on his stepson, knocking the knife loose.

Then he bolted for the back door. Kevin grabbed him from behind and wrestled him to the floor. Convinced his chest had been opened up, Ralston thought he'd be no match for Kevin, who was enraged and beating him up while still struggling to get closer to the knife. Confused, Ralston looked up at Kevin.

"You're trying to kill me?" he asked.

Kevin, his face red from the struggle, looked him in the eye. "Yes," he said, " . . . yes, that's what I want to do."

At that point, Ralston realized he'd die if he didn't get away. He summoned all of his strength and managed to wrestle Kevin off him and down to the floor. He got up and ran. Kevin tackled him, brought him down, but failed to immobilize him. He grabbed his stepdad by the calves, shouting: "You're not going out there; you're going to die right here." In the struggle, the button on Ralston's pants popped open. As he was wriggling out of them, and Kevin's grasp, he struggled towards the front door. Kevin, sensing he was losing his grip, shouted to Pierre: "Kill him! Kill him! Kill him!"

Up until this point, Pierre had been watching, stunned, as Kevin attacked Ralston, just as Tim had when Kevin hacked away at Johnathon. He stood, open-mouthed with the wooden baseball bat in his hands, shocked at what he'd seen, both here and in the basement. But something in the urgency of Kevin's demand woke him out of his trance.

He pulled the bat behind his head and swung it at the prone man's head as hard as he could. He did it again and again. Ralston held his hand up in the air, trying to protect his bruised, bleeding head. He looked Pierre in the eye and said: "Why are you doing this to me? I've never done anything to you." The only answer Pierre could provide was a tearful "I'm sorry, I'm sorry, I'm sorry," and took a few more whacks at him.

Desperate, Ralston kept struggling. He wriggled out of his pants and crawled to the front door. Behind him, he heard Kevin yell: "Jesus Christ! He's getting away!" Ralston managed to open the door and screamed for help. He noticed Pierre position himself on the stairway so he could hit him with the bat again. Kevin shut the front door, but Ralston kept screaming. With one more push, Ralston managed to open the door just enough for him to squeeze through. He lost his pants and jacket in the process.

Clad in just boxer shorts and a T-shirt despite the snow, and with blood dripping from his head, Ralston kept screaming. Unaware if anyone could hear him, he yelled: "Please help, They're trying to kill me!" Luckily, a woman happened to be riding by the house on her bicycle exactly as he escaped. He stopped her and shouted, "Please help me! They're trying to kill me!" She rode to a payphone and called 911.

Ralston ran to a nearby house, where he knew the residents. He recounted the story and the neighbors called 911 again. The calls were logged in at 5:39 and 5:42 p.m.

As soon as Pierre and Kevin saw Ralston and the bicyclist leave, they fled the house. Taking nothing—not even their weapons—with them, and with no more complicated plan than simply running away, they sprinted as fast and as far as their legs and lungs would allow.

* * *

Detective Glenn Gray began to listen to the tape Ashley and her friends had made. He had heard hundreds of death threats before, but was particularly unnerved and even a little sickened by this one. He later told me he "had never heard a tape so cold and calculated." These kids were talking about murder as casually as someone else might talk about their day at the office.

He was about halfway through it when another cop asked him if he'd just sent some officers to an address on Dawes. He said that he had and the other officer told him about the two calls for an attempted murder at No. 90.

Within seconds, Gray ordered an emergency task force (ETF) to 90 Dawes. They were heavily armed and specially trained in assault and negotiation techniques, but they didn't know who was inside the house, what they were armed with, and if they had any hostages or not. Gray also ordered more discreet teams to the addresses he had been given for Tim, Pierre and Ashley.

He then called Ashley's house. He told her parents that the two big guys in the car parked in front of her house were his men and that they were there for their protection. If the phone should ring, he told them, pick it up, but don't let any of the boys speak with Ashley under any circumstances. If Tim or any of the boys should come banging on the door, Gray told them to call him and he'd have his men in the car arrest him.

The ETF arrived at 90 Dawes at 6:30. They stationed a team out front, but the bulk of the men entered through the smaller, weaker back door. Once they determined that the house was secure, they searched the place. It didn't take long to find Johnathon. The ETF team followed the sloppy trail of blood smeared on the floor and walls that started at the pool at the bottom of the stairs, went through the broken glass the boys had dragged him over and up to the tiny crawlspace they'd jammed him into, intending it to be his final resting place. The team saw his feet, with socks but no shoes, sticking out. They called to him. He didn't answer. An officer opened the blood-smeared door and found Johnathon inside, his body in a fetal position and covered in blood.

Despite their training and experience with grisly matters, the officers who found Johnathon were shocked and sickened at their discovery. Crimes against children do tend to have more profound effects on police officers and the sight of Johnathon's body, twisted and mashed to fit in the miserable little hole he was stuffed into, his face and throat covered in blood, horrified the officers present. At first, they hoped he was still alive.

The officers immediately called for paramedics.

* * *

Meanwhile, Tim had fled for home by bus. Seeing Ralston arrive had really spooked him. He vainly hoped that nobody would ever find Johnathon, who he and Kevin had shoved—still weakly fighting for breath—into the tiny crawlspace. He hoped that it would all just go away. He didn't think about the ridiculous amount of forensic evidence they'd left behind. He didn't think about whether Johnathon would live or die.

He'd been on the bus for one stop when it opened its doors again to take on two bloodstained youths. The other passengers on the bus did their best to ignore Kevin and Pierre as they shambled toward the back of the bus out of habit. They sat near, but not with, Tim. He looked at Kevin. The big boy nodded, but did not speak. Kevin and Pierre got off after two stops and walked into the woods of Taylor Creek Ravine.

But Tim didn't think that much of it at the time. All he could think about was Ashley. He thought about how beautiful she was, how much he loved her, and how he hoped that she would provide him with the comfort he was sure he couldn't get anywhere else.

When the bus finally stopped at the corner nearest his apartment, Tim ran home and straight up to his room. At 5:55, he called Ashley and got her father. Keeping in mind what Gray had told him, her father told Tim that Ashley wasn't home, but perhaps he should try again a little later. Ashley's dad later described the boy's demeanor as nervous, but unfailingly polite.

For almost an hour, Tim did nothing more than pace around the Ferrimans' small apartment and worry. He called Ashley again at 6:41. Her dad answered again. He lied again, telling Tim that Ashley was still out with her friends, but that he expected her home at any minute.

* * *

At 6:55, the paramedics arrived at 90 Dawes and raced down to the basement. They replaced the cops in the tiny crawlspace. As soon as they got there, they could see Johnathon was, as paramedics say, VSA (vital signs absent). They wrapped Johnathon's body in a specially designed blanket and rushed him outside. Once he was inside the ambulance, the paramedics rapidly tried to clamp off all his leaking blood vessels and massage his heart. One of the paramedics, attempting to intubate him, shone a light down his mouth to guide the tube. He was shocked to see the light reflected on the opposite wall—it was coming out of the holes in Johnathon's throat.

At 7:07, on the sidewalk just in front of 90 Dawes, inside the ambulance—after all life-saving avenues were exhausted—Johnathon was declared dead.

* * *

Gray, informed that none of the suspects were still inside the house, sent a part of the ETF to Tim's address. Armed with shotguns, they surrounded both entrances to the second-floor apartment and called inside. There was no answer. Tim had the phone in his hand when it rang, and he hoped it would be Ashley. But he let it ring, just in case it wasn't.

He knew that if he got in touch with her, there were things he wanted to say to her that he didn't want his father to hear. So at 7:35, Tim walked to the apartment's back door and hesitated at the top of the steps into the back yard with the portable phone in his hand. Although Tim hadn't yet taken a step outside, the members of the ETF could clearly see him through the open door. He didn't realize it at first, but he had more than a dozen guns aimed at his head.

The cops yelled at him, told him to stop moving, to put the phone down. He didn't. They shouted the order at him again and again. Still he refused. He later claimed he couldn't hear them. After waiting for a response from Tim, one cop ran up to him and kicked him in the chest. Tim crumpled and the cops cuffed him and placed him under arrest.

The commotion drew the attention of Tim's ailing father—also named Tim Ferriman—who came outside to see what was the matter. When Tim saw him, he told him: "Dad, I witnessed a murder." Enraged at seeing his son roughly handled and on the ground, the older Ferriman began to argue with and threaten several police officers. He was quickly placed under arrest.

As police led young Tim Ferriman down the stairs, he passed by ETF leader James Hung, recognized that he was in charge, and told him: "I know why you guys are here; I know what this is all about." He started talking as soon as the arresting officer read him his right to counsel. On the drive to the police station, the officers questioned him about the whereabouts of Kevin and Pierre. He provided police with detailed descriptions of the two boys, including where they were and what they were wearing when he last saw them.

When he was brought to 54 Division, Tim was allowed to explain to his father what had happened in private. His father was then released without being charged.

The officers there took Tim at his word and were treating him like a witness to an attempted murder. That changed when Gray arrived. When he saw Tim waiting around the station, barely supervised, he told the officers there that he wasn't a witness, but a suspect. "He's in this," he told them. Tim was quickly taken into more secure custody.

Despite appearing willing to talk in the car, Tim changed his mind at the police station and decided to wait for a lawyer. Aware that they would get no more information from him that night, the police offered him the chance to make a phone call. Unlike in the United States, a prisoner's one phone call is not a guaranteed right in Canada, but it has become customary over the years. Excited, Tim told them he wanted to call Ashley. They refused.

* * *

At 8:00 p.m., Joanne—unaware that her son was dead—finished up her shift at a popular chain restaurant and headed for home. She got off the subway at the Main Street stop, as she had thousands of times before, and walked the two blocks east to Dawes. She could see flashing lights in the dark sky, but didn't think much about it. It wasn't exactly a high-crime area, but things happened there from time to time and a few flashing lights in the neighborhood didn't overly concern her. As soon as Joanne turned the corner, though, she saw just how many police cars there were and how big the crowds were. As she got closer, she could tell they were in front of her house. She broke into a run. By the time she got to the police line, she was frantic and screaming. Once the police and other emergency personnel identified her as Johnathon's mother, they surrounded her, separated her from the curious onlookers, packed her in the back seat of a car and took her away for debriefing and grief counseling.

Another family member, who can't be identified, returning home from a friend's house shortly after Joanne arrived, ignored the police and emergency staff, lifted up the yellow police tape and walked up to the front door. When stopped by a police officer, the person in question calmly said, "Oh, it's okay; I live here."

* * *

At about the same time that Joanne found out that her son was dead—and that it was probably her other son who had murdered him—the forensic examiner finished the preliminary report on Johnathon's battered body. After all the blood and other tissue were cleaned off, the doctor counted no fewer than 71 entry wounds from a large, bladed weapon. Almost all of them were around the face or throat. One thrust—the one that probably killed him—cut so deep that it took a small chunk out of Johnathon's backbone.

* * *

After Tim gave his initial statements and told him he wouldn't speak further without a lawyer present, Gray decided they needed to hear more from Ashley and her friends that night. He had his staff bring them all in. It was about 10:00 p.m. when they were finally all assembled. He sat them all in a conference room. Each girl had one or both of her parents with her. They all struck him as nice, polite, even upstanding young women. He was saddened that he had to break the news to them.

"Some of what you heard on the tape today came true," he told them. They all screamed and cried, some even fell to the floor. It was only then that Ashley learned Kevin's little brother's name was Johnathon and that he was 12, not five as she'd imagined, and that he was dead.

* * *

Kevin and Pierre didn't get very far that night. While the police searched the area, the boys hid in Taylor Creek Park, which starts just a few blocks north of 90 Dawes.

Although it's big, there's not much to the park: just a creek, some marshes and a few trails cut into the lightly wooded ravine. Torontonians appreciate the city's many wooded valleys for a chance to get closer to nature and away from the city's hustle and bustle. But Taylor Creek isn't one of Toronto's more popular ravines; not many people go there and almost none ever show up at night. When there's even a light dusting of snow on the ground—as there was November 25, 2003—it can be an eerily quiet place.

Kevin and Pierre, familiar with the park from many smoking and drinking sessions, had no problem staying hidden from the few flashlight beams that penetrated the trees in search of them. They stayed the night there without incident.

The following day, police officers were combing the neighborhood looking for the boys. A call came in from a person who recognized Kevin and Tim from images shown on TV that morning. Because both suspects were under 18, the police needed to get a judge's permission to release their photos to the media. The witness had seen not only the boys, but also the blood on their clothes.

Detective Constables Chris Sherk and Erin Bradshaw spotted Pierre at the corner of Coxwell Ave. and O'Connor Drive—a busy intersection about two-and-a-half miles away from 90 Dawes. Sherk later said he was surprised to see the most-wanted fugitives in the country "just strolling around" out in the open. Sherk stopped his car and apprehended Pierre. As he "took physical control" of the skinny 6-foot, maybe 140-pound boy, Sherk told him he was under arrest for murder. Pierre shrugged and indicated that he understood. Sherk was perplexed by the lack of concern the boy showed.

As Sherk was taking Pierre down, Detective Sergeants John Rossano and Chris Haynes arrived from another direction after recognizing Kevin, who was on a different side of the same corner as Pierre. Rossano leapt from his car to arrest the big boy. And he too was surprised at how calm the murder suspect was. Kevin was not only giving no resistance, but he was showing no emotion. Rossano asked him: "Do you understand what this is about?" Kevin nodded and replied: "Yeah, the death of my brother." Both arrests were recorded at 2:35 p.m., November 26.

Despite—or maybe because of—the seriousness of the situation, the cops at intake couldn't help but feel a mordant amusement when they saw what the boys were wearing. Kevin had on a bright red T-shirt with the Nike slogan "Just Do It," and Pierre was wearing a white T-shirt with a picture of a man up to his neck in the Nile River just in front of the pyramids, with the words "Deep In Denial" printed beneath him.

* * *

Later that day, homicide Detective Sergeant Terry Wark and his partner Jerry Ball were brought in to interrogate Kevin. Before he turned the tape recorder on, Wark told Kevin that he and Ball were both fathers and that they were trying very hard to understand why he'd done what he had. Kevin offered no response. Wark informed him that he could talk to a lawyer before he answered any questions. He also repeated the charges against him. Kevin said he understood. They began the interview when Wark turned on the tape.

Wark: Do you wish to say anything in answer to the charges against you?
Kevin: I want to say it was not first degree; I didn't plan it.

That response surprised Wark, but he surmised that Kevin was trying to play Canada's *Youth Criminal Justice Act* (formerly named, and still better known as, the *Young Offenders Act*) to his advantage. Under the controversial and much-criticized legislation, Wark anticipated that Kevin was aware that he would face a much lighter sentence if tried as a youth than he would as an adult and that he would probably not be tried as an adult unless the charge was first-degree murder.

At that point, Kevin asked if could call a lawyer. Wark agreed and turned off the tape. Then Kevin returned to the interrogation room and Wark turned the tape back on.

Wark: Do you realize what you've done?
Kevin: Yes I do.
Wark: How do you feel?
Kevin: Not so good.
Wark: What did your brother do to deserve to die?

At this point, Kevin began to cry.

Kevin: I just get depressed . . . and things happen . . . and I snap . . .
Wark: Why your little brother?
Kevin: I don't want to talk about it.

Kevin regained his composure.

Wark: Anything else to say?
Kevin: No.
Wark: Any further questions?
Kevin: No.

CHAPTER 3

# the truth about goths: why kids want to be vampires

About a week after Johnathon's death, Ashley received an alarming e-mail. She was very surprised to see that it was from Tim. The subject line was—as was usual for Tim—typed in all caps and with little regard for spelling or grammar, it read: IM IN JAIL.

Tim was being held at the Syl Apps Youth and Secure Treatment Centre. Kevin and Pierre were at other facilities. The Syl Apps Centre is in Oakville, Ontario, about an hour's drive southwest of 90 Dawes. Named after the late star forward for the Toronto Maple Leafs and Olympic pole-vaulter who later became a Conservative Member of Parliament, the Syl Apps is a detention, custody and treatment facility for mentally ill youth.

Normally it is an efficiently run facility that has little interaction with the neighborhood around it, and it has been the source of few news-making incidents. But on December 1, 2003, Tim was left unsupervised on an Internet-equipped computer long enough to log onto his MSN e-mail account and compose a message for Ashley. The message was time-stamped at around midnight, but my sources tell me that the kids at Syl Apps frequently change times and dates on the computers there just for fun, and it was most likely sent in the early afternoon. At least, that's when Ashley received it.

"This is the story," was his opener, and he went on to claim that none of what happened was his fault. He explained to her that when he arrived at Kevin's, he and Pierre were already talking about killing Kevin's family. Since they were laughing and having a good time, he was sure they were joking and so he went along with the joke. As he understood it, Kevin was planning to run away from home that day because of problems with his stepfather, and all the talk of killing his family was just his fantasizing out loud.

But as Kevin began to get more destructive in the house, Tim claimed he became more and more frightened of him—frightened even for his own life. He became even more scared when Johnathon came home. According to the note, Kevin and Pierre were determined to beat Johnathon up, but Tim intervened, suggesting that they merely threaten the boy instead.

But after Kevin threw his little brother down the stairs, Tim wrote, he was so scared he couldn't even move. And when Kevin told Tim to go get him a butcher knife from the kitchen, he said he complied without thinking.

Tim then made it clear that it was Kevin alone, and not him, who hacked Johnathon to death. Tim closed his message with a rather beseeching: "Please, I wouldn't do that you have to believe me."

It was a far cry from the young man who was almost blasé while bragging about murdering strangers and drinking their blood.

As soon as she finished reading the message, Ashley called detective Glenn Gray.

* * *

Dahlia (not her real name) is meeting with me to tell me about Tim. She wouldn't come to meet me alone. Something about seeing a much older man she met over the Internet spooks her, so she arrives at the coffee shop with a phalanx of four friends. After introductions—I give her a copy of *Fallen Angel*, my first book, to establish a little credibility—we sit at a booth in the back and the rest of her crew sits at a table about ten feet away. I'd rather they were farther away because if she knows they can hear her, it may prejudice her answers, but they won't budge.

From first impressions, she doesn't appear to have much in common with Ashley. She's short and small-featured and looks much younger than her 18 years. She's more cute than pretty and does not project a great deal of self-confidence. She has an appearance of vulnerability Ashley doesn't share. Dahlia's hair is not quite shoulder length and blonde. It's an unnatural color that suits neither her eyes nor her complexion.

She tells me it's not what she looked like when she dated Tim. Back then, it was dyed black (her long-abandoned natural color is, she says, "mouse brown" and she absolutely hates it). And back then she wore white foundation with heavy black mascara and eyeliner, rather than the subtle, girl-next-door look she goes with now.

When I ask her about Tim, she says she wants to make it very clear she was never really into him. "Well, not exactly 'dated' dated," she corrects herself. "We went a few places and talked—it's not like we were boyfriend and girlfriend." In fact, that's why they broke up. I ask for details.

"It's a long story," she tells me. "I wore black, he wore black, so people naturally thought we should be together." According to Dahlia, when Tim came to her high school, nobody knew him, but her friends noticed him right away and were excited that there was a guy in school who looked and acted so much like her. Before long, they were pressuring her to get to know him; one friend of hers actually called them "a match made in hell."

So Dahlia did her best to get noticed by Tim and, before long, he built up enough courage to talk to her and eventually to ask her out. They didn't do much. He never seemed to have any money; so most of their dates consisted of just walking and talking. They spoke even more often electronically. Besides hanging around at school, they also communicated through e-mail and by MSN Instant Messenger at night.

She tells me that it wouldn't have bothered her that they didn't go anywhere—she likes talking—but he didn't really have anything to talk about. He was boring. He was always around, always talking, but never seemed to have anything to say. Once they discussed what their favorite bands were, there wasn't all that much left to talk about. And it bothered her that she called her his girlfriend. "I mean," she tells me. "All we did was walk around together."

And it bothered her that he was so immature. He would frequently affect accents or talk in the voices of his favorite cartoon characters. It was annoying, but not as annoying as the smug grin he had on his face whenever he said or did something he thought was funny. "Which was constantly," she said.

She was thinking about breaking it off with him when he made her mind up for her. On one of their nighttime walks, he stopped, turned to face her, held both of her hands and told her he loved her. That's when she knew she was done with him. She told him so. He started yelling and screaming and even punched a wall. He cried. She relented and told him she'd see him the next day, but that she wasn't really interested in being his girlfriend.

The next time they got together, Tim got her alone and told her that he'd been acting funny because he had a secret, a secret he could tell only her.

It was, she tells me in the coffee shop, a difficult moment for her. Although she was annoyed at Tim and not at all interested in dating him anymore, she certainly didn't dislike him and if he had a real problem, she didn't want to abandon him. A few things ran through her mind. She knew he wasn't gay. It could be drugs—maybe someone was out to get him for money he owed. She stopped walking, eager to listen, perhaps to help.

Tim turned around to face her, grabbed both her hands as he did earlier when he told her he loved her, looked her straight in the eyes and told her that he was a vampire and that he drank human blood.

At the coffee shop, she gives me a look that clearly says, "Can you believe it?"

I nod, roll my eyes and ask her what she did next.

Shocked that he would say something so ridiculous, so stupid, she jerked her hands back and told him she never wanted to see him again. And then she walked away. At home, she blocked his instant messages and refused to open his e-mails.

"I should've slapped him," she tells me. "He had me worried for a minute there."

I ask her what happened after that.

"Well," she says, "he eventually kind of got the message and stopped bothering me." After a while she started saying "hi" to him again (after she heard he was seeing someone else) when they saw each other in school, but that was about it.

I ask her why the vampire thing bothered her so much; was it just that she expected something else? "Well, mostly," she tells me. "But I also felt like I was being played." She confesses that she was, at the time, a Goth. Goths, she explains, are kids who dress up in black and lots of makeup and try to look spooky. They listen to darkly themed music and tend to like things related to horror movies and other scary things like bats, spiders and ravens. But because she was a Goth, she believes Tim assumed that she was interested in vampires and drinking blood for real.

"That stuff's disgusting," she says. "Just because I wore all black doesn't mean I want to kill people and drink their blood."

It's actually a lot of fun, she assures me, to be a Goth, to look different than everyone else. She was a Goth, she says, simply because she likes dressing up and because she thought the music was cool.

"So why aren't you a Goth anymore?" I ask.

"Because there are so many jerks out there who take it too seriously," she says. "Tim's not the only one, you meet them on the Net all the time—they all think they're real live vampires—it's just not fun anymore."

* * *

"Are vampires real?"

I was putting my seven-year-old son to bed when he asked that. He must have heard me talking about the book.

"No, vampires are an old legend from a faraway place a long time ago," I told him. He looked at me as though he expected more, so I oblige. "People like to make up scary stories like that because it gets them all excited and then, when they realize everything's okay and there's nothing to be scared about, it makes them feel all better." He decided my explanation sounded plausible enough and went off to sleep.

I wasn't exactly telling the truth. While it's true that the original legend—that of the dead awakening, hungering for the blood of the living to keep them from a permanent grave—is nothing more than a twisted fairy tale that parents used hundreds of years ago to terrify their children into obedience, there actually are vampires out there.

To be more precise, there are people—lots of them—who call themselves vampires. And some of them actually do drink blood. They show up every once in a while on *Jerry Springer*-style shows. Tim must have thought they were kind of cool, because he repeatedly told people he was one of them.

It's a bizarre take on history, actually. People grow up with the idea that vampires are cool, erotic and dangerous. And for various reasons—psychologists note a lack of guidance from parents, a contextual skew caused by an early exposure to media intended for adults, and a lack of social structure—some teens acquire an indistinct or totally misdirected opinion about what's real and what isn't. They become vampires, at least in the sense that they drink blood and say they are vampires, because they want very badly to *be* vampires.

This doesn't surprise the experts. Lynn Schofield Clark—psychologist and author of *From Angels to Aliens: Teenagers, the Media and the Supernatural*—makes the following points about teens in our culture:

> • [North] American culture is so steeped in Judeo-Christian heritage; teens must make options that fit the mold of that tradition. Vampires, as a long-standing European myth, are part of that background.
>
> • While teens are media-savvy, their ability to make distinctions between entertainment, culture, fact and religion is easily blurred, leading to an "openness to possibility" philosophy, which allows them to accept things they see portrayed in media as truth, if they are presented realistically. Without a larger frame of reference to draw upon, teens may be unable to separate metaphor from fact. Clark notes cross-genre TV shows like *Buffy the Vampire Slayer*, *Charmed* and *Touched by an Angel* that may cause spiritual confusion.
>
> • Teens may adopt a form of spiritual belief other than that of their parents or peers to affect rebellion, or may simply be dissatisfied with the dominant spiritual beliefs (or lack of them) around them and look for something else.

That Tim Ferriman told people he was a vampire may surprise some, but it's not actually that uncommon. In fact, there are many thousands of people his age all over the world who dress up like vampires, and a few who drink blood.

But those few generally don't actually attack people in the night and bite their necks, the self-described vampires I met told me. Instead, they usually depend on friends and each other to supply them with blood.

I asked a psychologist friend of mine who deals with teenagers on a regular basis why some of them dressed up like vampires, rather than, say, cowboys or pirates. "That's an easy one," he told me. "Cowboys and pirates were real and can be judged in historical context; since no real vampires ever existed, they can't be judged—as a result, these kids are free to make up their mythology as they go along."

He's right.

"Besides," he adds, "cowboys and pirates are just people, with all the frailties that implies. Vampires are magical beings, which some kids who are looking for a way to differentiate themselves from the larger group find extra appealing."

He thinks about it a bit longer and says, "who knows, it could have been cowboys or pirates if some kids started dressing that way—but it was vampires."

He's talking about the Goth movement that came out of England in the early 1980s. If you aren't aware of Goths, you're in a distinct minority. For almost 30 years, legions of kids have been dyeing their hair black, wearing black often anachronistic clothes, putting on heavy makeup and listening to doom-and-gloom music.

Although most sources tell me there aren't as many of them as there once were, it's hard to find a high school in Europe, North America, or Australia that doesn't have at least a few.

Canada, and Toronto in particular, seems to have a disproportionate number. It started, I'm told by a number of sources (including Goths themselves, music journalists, police, mental health professionals and others), with a group of kids who hung out on Toronto's Queen Street West in the middle 1980s. Trends tend to hit Canada later than they do in Europe and the United States, and aficionados of what was then called "new music"—punk, new wave, new romantic and just about anything other than what's now called "classic rock"—were few in number, not very popular in the mainstream community, and they tended to seek each other out. Before long, they began meeting informally on Queen Street—primarily between University and Spadina. The location offered lots of foot traffic for panhandling (some of them were homeless and many more jobless) and many bars with live music and cheap draft beer. Because passersby often referred to them as "freaks," the Queen Street kids took the name as a badge of honor.

As more and more teens became fans of alternative music—thanks in a large part to Queen Street's own live music venues and the MuchMusic

music TV network, whose storefront headquarters had been located at Queen and John since 1984—the Freaks grew in number and splintered into various sets. By 1987, the Goths, with their vampire-like fashions, were frequenting their own hangouts and eventually had their own bars and nightclubs.

The movement peaked after a dance club called Sanctuary: The Vampire Sex Bar opened in September 1992. Fashionably, it was located on Queen Street across from a Centre for Addiction and Mental Health facility. The club imposed a strict "Goth dress only" entry requirement. It was consistently very popular and drew many from the Toronto Goth scene, including those too young to get into clubs farther east on Queen, on the other side of Bathurst. Demand for a place to "be" became so strong among teenagers that the club also opened for underage Goths twice a week. The money lost on liquor sales was more than recouped by gate receipts, once a cover charge was installed.

But the Goth scene began to decline in numbers in the mid-1990s. Some cite unfavorable media coverage, while others say that Goth culture was co-opted by more mainstream acts like Marilyn Manson. Still others say that these days, Goths spend more time on the Internet than they do at nightclubs. As other bars in the Queen West area began offering "Goth nights," Sanctuary closed its doors.

In a move that infuriated the area's Goths, Sanctuary's owners sold out to the giant Starbucks coffee shop chain in 2000. When the coffee bar opened a few months later, the owners held an opening night gala in which they invited customers to "come dressed in your best Goth attire" to try some free coffee drinks.

But a significant vestige of the Goth district remains around Queen and Bathurst. It now consists of three dedicated dance clubs (ironically, two of them—Savage Garden and Velvet Underground—share names with decidedly non-Goth bands), some boutiques and a few dozen kids dressed in black hanging around outside them all.

In an effort to better understand Goth, vampires and the forces that molded Tim Ferriman and people like him, I visited them all, interviewed people on the street and online and even opened up a few history books.

* * *

The original Goths were a tribe of people who emerged from the east to attack the Roman Empire circa 263 A.D. What they did before that and where they came from are a matter of mystery and conjecture. After meeting up with, and raiding the edges of, the weakening Roman Empire, the Goths set up a nation-state of sorts in Dacia (modern-day Romania), which the Romans had abandoned as unprofitable a few years earlier.

They developed a more-or-less friendly trading relationship with the nearby Byzantines. After Byzantium was conquered by the Romans, becoming Nova Roma (New Rome), and then Constantinople (known today as Istanbul, Turkey), the Goths became increasingly Romanized. Most of them spoke at least a little Latin, they adopted the rudiments of Roman-style government and dress and their state religion, Christianity.

The Goths divided themselves into two distinct groups—the Ostrogoths and Visigoths. Although the Romans thought the names meant "eastern Goths" and "western Goths," both "ostro" and "visi" basically meant "good" in the Gothic language, so a modern translation would be more like "excellent Goths" and "awesome Goths."

Under severe pressure from another proto-European tribe, the Huns, the Ostrogoths asked the Romans for permission to cross the Danube and settle in the Empire under Roman protection. In exchange for land and grain, the Ostrogoths were expected to act as a buffer zone between the Romans and the Huns.

It worked out pretty well for both sides until a major famine hit the Empire in 376. The Romans cut the Ostrogoths' grain rations to nothing, but continued supplying the Roman garrisons in the area as usual. When the starving Ostrogoths appealed to the garrisons for help, they were offered dog meat in exchange for female slaves.

Enraged, the Ostrogoths marched to the nearest major Roman city, Marcianopolis in what is now Bulgaria. Many of their sick, children, elderly and even healthy adult women died along the way, leaving them largely a band of very angry and desperate young men. When they arrived at Marcianopolis, they were barred from the walled city, and the local governors clumsily attempted to assassinate the Ostrogoths' leaders at a hastily arranged summit meeting.

At that point, the Ostrogoths decided the Romans were their enemies, and that they had nothing left to lose. Avoiding the undermanned Roman garrisons in the area, the Ostrogoths raided and looted the countryside at will, taking everything they could from the largely defenseless local people. When the Romans stood idly by, the Goths were encouraged by their success and drew reinforcements from locals eager to get rid of their Imperial overlords. The rebellious Ostrogoths managed to occupy much of what is now Bulgaria, Eastern Greece and the European part of Turkey.

The Romans sent a military expedition under the command of Emperor Valens himself to put down the revolt. It didn't work. At the Battle of Adrianople in 378, the combination of a strong Gothic cavalry charge and a group of over-eager Romans who attacked before they were ordered to do so led to an impressive rout by the Goths. Valens, abandoned by his guards, was killed in the ensuing massacre.

The very idea of a barbarian tribe defeating a Roman army—let alone killing the Emperor—was absolutely unthinkable, and the area collapsed into chaos. The Ostrogoths and their allies began to ravage the Balkans, killing Roman administrators and destroying Imperial infrastructure.

The Romans eventually responded, pushing the Ostrogoths to negotiate a peaceful settlement with Valens' successor Theodosius in 382. But the Ostrogoths had made a powerful point. The so-called barbarian tribes surrounding the Roman Empire had gained enough technology, discipline and will to take on the Romans and win—it was the beginning of the end of the Empire.

After the peace agreement, the Ostrogoths were ostensibly allies of the Empire again, but mutinies and looting raids against the Romans became commonplace. Eventually the Ostrogoths allied with other tribes—including the fearsome Vandals, Huns and Alans—to commit opportunistic, small-scale invasions around the Empire's edges.

Emboldened by the success of his distant relatives, Alaric, king of the Visigoths, attacked Italy. Although he was defeated in battle twice by the legendary Roman general Flavius Stilicho, he survived and remained a threat to the Empire. The Emperor Honorious actually moved the Empire's capital from Rome to the distant city of Ravenna out of fear. Foolishly, he also had Stilicho executed on trumped-up charges of plotting a coup. With his formidable adversary out of the picture, Alaric invaded Italy and his men laid siege to Rome in 410. Rather than fight, Honorious offered to pay the Visigoths to leave. Alaric accepted and gave the Romans 300 slaves as a sign of goodwill.

The Romans accepted the slaves and then refused to pay. In a move as cunning as the more famous Trojan Horse ruse, the Visigoth "slaves" then fought their way to the Salarian Gate and let their allies into the walled city—and the sack of Rome began. The Visigoths looted Rome for three days.

Although they didn't take all that much, the Visigoths' raid had a profound effect on the Empire. Rome, the Eternal City, had been safe from invaders for 800 years. But after its sacking by the Visigoths, barbarian raiders started pouring in and the Empire started to disintegrate.

However, the Goths had their own problems. Constantly attacked by neighboring tribes, they struggled to survive. The Ostrogoths were eventually defeated and absorbed by the Longobards in Italy in 568, while the Visigoths were beaten and dispersed by the Ummayyads in Spain in 711.

Later Europeans, particularly in Spain and Sweden, claimed to be descendants of Goths, but they really didn't exist as an identifiable people after the eighth century.

While the Goths undeniably have a place in history for their part in the fall of the Roman Empire, few people really identify with them anymore. It's not as though teenagers dress up in barbarian finery when they call themselves Goths. In fact, the word "Goth" was for many centuries an insult, suggesting a lack of refinement or intellect—a barbaric mentality, quite the opposite of how today's "Goths" like to view themselves.

The word's meaning has changed over the centuries, like many do, as a result of ignorance and, in this case, something of a scam. Horace Walpole was an eighteenth century English nobleman, politician, poet and architect. He called his broad, strong architectural style "gothic," to differentiate it from the much more detailed neo-classical style that was popular in his time. His style didn't have much in common with what the Goths actually built (virtually none of which still existed by his time), but few people questioned the authenticity of the term. Besides, Walpole's buildings looked old, and gothic was a cool, old-sounding word, so it stuck.

Walpole had clearly grown attached to the name, because when he wrote his first novel, *The Castle of Otranto,* in 1764, he described it as "gothic." Walpole said he had found a long-forgotten Italian manuscript dating from 1529 in a library of an "ancient Catholic family in the North of England." He said he had meticulously translated the story, which itself was a retelling of a far older story from the days of the barbarians, and released it as a "gothic" novel. A long, violent tale that involved prophecy, ghosts, monsters and other supernaturalia, *The Castle of Otranto* was also heavily laden with eroticism and sexual innuendo.

Not surprisingly, it was a huge success and went into many printings. Although Walpole later relented and admitted he had written the book, it didn't make much difference. The addictive blend of supernatural violence mixed with subtle eroticism had already become known as the gothic style.

Walpole's success launched countless imitators and, even centuries later, many are inspired by his style. But the best known gothic novel is, of course, Bram Stoker's *Dracula*.

An Irish immigrant, Stoker worked hard and eventually became business manager of the world famous Lyceum Theatre in London. While there, he earned extra money and became quite well connected by writing sensational novels—what we'd call pulp fiction today. While researching his books, Stoker became quite interested in Eastern European legends, particularly that of the vampire.

Although stories of the dead rising to eat the flesh and blood of the living are commonplace in most Western cultures, including those of the ancient Greeks and Romans, the vampire legend we know today originated in Southeastern Europe, including Transylvania—the northern part of Romania, where it borders Hungary.

Although there were significant and often bizarre regional differences—Albanian vampires were said to have a preference for high-heeled shoes, while a Bulgarian one could be identified by his single nostril—the armature of the story was surprisingly consistent throughout much of the region. Vampires were dead humans who rose at night to drink the blood of living humans. Blood gave them strength and warded off a permanent grave. They feared and hated sunlight, and they could only be killed by esoteric means, including a stake to the heart or decapitation.

Stoker became intrigued, as he saw the potential for both horror and sexuality in the blood-sucking undead. He also wanted to play on the rising current of fear of foreigners that was then plaguing much of the British Empire. He knew he needed a compelling, charismatic nobleman as the lead character. An avid student of European history, Stoker settled on a combination of two notorious men, Gilles de Rais and Vlad Tepes.

De Rais was a fifteenth century French nobleman who used his position, good looks and abundant charm to get away with murder. He did get away with it for years, until he was implicated in the disappearance of a local priest who he'd been seen arguing with. Investigators discovered in his castle the remains of between 80 and 200 children, mostly boys, who de Rais had tortured, raped and murdered (often not in that order). His two henchmen told the complete story of how de Rais sent them to recruit the youngsters, ranging in age anywhere from 6 to 18, for him to have his deadly way with. The trio were hanged in 1440 and de Rais has since become identified as the first modern serial killer.

Tepes, on the other hand, was (and still is) to many people something of a hero. Although his father, Vlad II, was King of Wallachia (approximately the southern half of modern-day Romania), Vlad was born in Transylvania after his father was exiled by powerful Wallachian nobles loyal to the mighty Ottoman Empire. The second of three sons, Vlad III was later given by his father to the Turkish sultan as part of deal to stave off an Ottoman invasion.

Vlad hated his life as a captive and was frequently beaten for his insolence and refusal to convert to Islam. He secretly vowed to make the Turks pay.

In 1447, Vlad II was discovered in Transylvania and assassinated by Wallachian knights. Fearing rebellion, the Turks invaded and placed Vlad III on the throne as a puppet ruler. It made sense at the time: he was the legitimate claimant to the throne after his older brother Mircea was blinded by iron stakes and buried alive by political rivals; he had lived for so long under the boot of Ottoman oppression, they believed, that he would be too timid to do anything but what they told him.

It might have worked if Wallachia hadn't been invaded later that year by John Hunyadi—the man who killed Vlad II—forcing Vlad III to flee to Hungary. Eventually, the Hungarians convinced Hunyadi that Vlad III was a valuable ally, so he was pardoned and brought back to Wallachia as a political advisor. And when Hunyadi died of plague in 1456, Vlad III succeeded him as king.

Vlad quickly decided that his primary purpose as king was to protect himself. He eliminated a number of his rivals by execution and greatly reduced the economic and political power of the unpopular and often cruel noblemen, known as *boyars*. This—along with his natural charisma, frequent appearances at public events and reputation for fairness—made him phenomenally popular among his people.

Vlad is said to have won many loyal Wallachian admirers by his reaction to a Turkish emissary who refused to take off his hat before an infidel. According to the story, he had his men nail the Turk's hat to his head, which many Wallachians found hilarious at the time.

Vlad III was relentless in hunting down political rivals—particularly members of the Danesti clan—and killing anyone of any political stripe who could possibly pose a threat to his reign. It was at this time that he became known as Vlad the Impaler, because his preferred method of execution was to place the victim on top of a long metal rod so that the point of the rod entered the victim's anus and he died slowly as the weight of the body pushed it down the rod.

Deciding it was time to get back at the much-hated but all-powerful Ottoman Empire, he stopped paying them tribute and signed a truce with the Turks' bitter rivals, the Hungarians. When a Turkish mission to assassinate him failed, Vlad III invaded their territory in what's now Serbia and killed 20,000 mostly innocent people, many of whom received his signature impaling.

Enraged, Sultan Mehmed II of Turkey sent in an invasion force five times the size of Vlad's 20,000-man army and chased him out of Wallachia, installing Vlad's hated younger brother, Radu the Handsome, on the throne. Soon, Vlad was captured in Transylvania and imprisoned by the Hungarians.

The Hungarians took it easy on him—particularly after he converted to Catholicism—and eventually freed him. He lived with his wife and son in Budapest, plotting his revenge. At least one (largely pro-Vlad) telling of the story maintains that he simply could not give up his favorite hobby and frequently captured birds and animals to torture and mutilate.

In 1475, he gathered a number of Hungarian, Transylvanian and Wallachian allies and marched on his old capital. Radu had died two years earlier and the Turks had installed a man named Besarab as king. On hearing of Vlad's approach, Besarab fled, and Vlad was crowned without a fight. Convinced that their job was done, his allies left him with just a token guard of loyal Wallachians.

It was a bad idea. The Wallachian boyars, still angry with Vlad, revolted, captured him and delivered him to the Turks. There are many different accounts of the circumstances leading up to Vlad's death (all cruel), but historical documents of the event agree that he was finally beheaded, his head was preserved in honey and delivered to the Turkish sultan, who placed it on a stake in his palace as proof that Vlad was actually dead.

One of the key indications that Stoker based his character on Vlad is the novel's title itself. Vlad II's bloodthirsty reputation earned him the title "Dracul"—contemporary Romanian for "devil" or "dragon"—and he bore the title proudly, styling himself as Vlad Dracul (Vlad the Devil) during his reign. When Vlad III burst onto the scene with even more bloodlust, he became known by the diminutive form—as Vlad Dracula, or Vlad the Little Devil.

So entrenched was the idea that Vlad was the basis of Dracula that two Romanian sites later became tourist attractions billed as "Dracula's Castle." Poenari Castle actually was inhabited by Vlad III for a few years because it was at the top of a treacherous canyon and almost impervious to attack. But that same remoteness led Vlad and other rulers to abandon it, and it fell into ruin at least three times. Most of the walls and some towers still stand, but Poenari Castle is now really little more than a weedy pile of old bricks that tourists have to climb up 1,859 nearly vertical stairs to see.

Bran Castle, on the other hand, is easy to get to and looks very much like a storybook castle. It draws hundreds of thousands of visitors—but it's not Dracula's castle. Although the locals will tell you Vlad lived there, there's no historical evidence that he did. He was held prisoner in its dungeon for two days when the Ottomans held sway in the region, so he did actually stay there. And you can actually buy "Dracula's" castle if you really want it. The Romanian government, under pressure from the rest of the European Union to right the wrongs of its Communist predecessors, gave Bran Castle back to its rightful owner in 2006. Dominic von Habsburg—a retired furniture designer from suburban North Salem, New York, who is usually too humble to point out he's also Archduke Dominic—has put the property up for sale. The asking price is about $82 million, but may go higher because he has told his lawyers he will only sell to those "who will treat the property and its history with appropriate respect."

Although a number of popular novels featuring vampires had already appeared by that time, none had the critical impact of *Dracula*. Originally published in 1897, *Dracula* tells the story of an English lawyer, John Harker, who is sent to Transylvania to handle a real estate transaction his bosses are undertaking with a count who lives there. On his arrival, Harker is immediately impressed with Count Dracula's wealth, charm and refinement. But when Dracula pays a little too much attention to a picture of his fiancée, Mina, Harker begins to wonder about the intentions of his host. Before long, he realizes he's a prisoner in Dracula's castle and disobeys his orders not to go out of his room at night. When he first emerges to explore the castle, Harker is set upon by three beautiful women. At first he's pretty happy, until he realizes they want to kill him. Dracula saves him at the last minute and sends him on his way back to London.

After he returns, a Russian ship carrying nothing but coffin-sized boxes of sand from Transylvania runs aground in England. The crew is missing and the captain's log recounts a harrowing tale of crew member after crew member disappearing. After the ship crashes, witnesses report seeing a large animal, perhaps a wolf, jump off and dash away into the woods.

Immediately afterwards, Dracula appears in England and re-enters Harker's life. The Transylvanian count starts paying an undue amount of attention to Mina and her attractive friend Lucy. Before long, Lucy falls seriously ill. One of her wealthy suitors calls in a specialist, professor Abraham Van Helsing from Amsterdam, to help her out. Van Helsing quickly determines that Lucy has been bitten by a vampire, but refuses to tell anyone about it for fear he won't be believed. Lucy dies. When Van Helsing and her trio of suitors visit her grave to prove his hypothesis, she emerges, attacks them and they kill her (again) by beheading her.

Dracula finds out about this and bites Mina. He then flees to Transylvania, followed by Van Helsing and others who manage to kill Dracula by slashing his throat and stabbing him in the heart. His death frees Mina from his power and she and John live happily ever after.

Despite rave reviews on both sides of the Atlantic, *Dracula* was only a middling commercial success. It was very popular with literary and academic types, but failed to catch on with a larger audience.

Realizing that Stoker's slow pacing and dense prose were *Dracula*'s inhibiting factors, an enterprising German filmmaker, Freidrich Wilhelm Murnau, decided to adapt the story for the screen in 1921. He had no trouble finding investors once he decided on a leading man. Max Schreck was a talented veteran stage actor whom Murnau described as "strikingly ugly"—and it didn't hurt that his family name coincidentally happened to be the German word for "terror."

Careful not to infringe on copyright, Murnau changed the name of the main character from Count Dracula to Graf (the German equivalent of count) Orlok and the title from Dracula to *Nosferatu*. Actually, the entire title was *Nosferatu, eine Symphonie des Grauens* (Nosferatu, Symphony of Horror). Murnau never explained the origin of the name, but *nosophoros* is Greek for "plague carrier" (Orlok does spread the plague in the movie) and *nesuferitul* is Romanian for "the insufferable one."

His precautions didn't work. In 1922, Florence Stoker, Bram's widow, received an anonymous package from Berlin. In it was a poster for *Nosferatu* that featured a line that read: "Freely adapted from Bram Stoker's *Dracula*." As diligent as Murnau was throughout the production, his promoters let him down after the film was made.

Florence set her lawyers upon Prana-Film GmbH, the company that produced *Nosferatu,* and obtained a cease-and-desist order. All prints of the film were ordered delivered to Florence to be destroyed, and Prana-Film, crippled by damage payments, went bankrupt before it could produce another film. Murnau, however, went on to great success, including a stint in Hollywood. His film *Wings*, about World War I fighter pilots, won the first-ever Oscar for best picture.

But the European legal authorities were not completely effective in suppressing the film. Nobody knows how they got there, but prints of *Nosferatu* had emerged in both New York and Detroit by 1929 and drew large audiences at unauthorized exhibitions. It still plays regularly (the copyright has lapsed), mostly to audiences of film students and hardcore vampire fans.

If you watch it now (plenty of people do; it's regarded as a landmark film), *Nosferatu* is quaint at best and hilarious at worst. But at the time, it was considered absolutely horrifying. There are many recorded reports of its viewers passing out in terror. The Swedish government actually outlawed it on the grounds of "excessive horror," and did not lift the ban until 1972.

Murnau has a reputation as an expressionist genius, but he seems to have missed the point of *Dracula* when he made *Nosferatu*. The movie is horrifying, sure, but the vampire is a terrifying creature with no redeeming qualities. He's a monster. Unlike the Dracula of the book, Orlok has no charm, no *savoir faire*. He's about as sexy as Leatherface from *The Texas Chainsaw Massacre*.

Movie audiences didn't see a deeper, more effective—truly gothic in the Walpolian sense—representation of Dracula on screen until 1931.

Harry Deane moved to London from Northern Ireland and supported himself by writing, acting in and producing small-scale stage plays. Aware of what had happened with *Nosferatu*, Deane sought Florence Stoker's permission to make a play based on *Dracula* in exchange for a cut of the profits. Deane had intended to play the count himself—he had already produced and played the part of the monster in *Frankenstein*—but decided that Van Helsing was a better role, leaving an actor named Richard Huntley to play the vampire.

His version of *Dracula* opened in 1924 in Derby and was a huge and immediate success, the like of which Deane had never seen before. It played London nonstop for three years and spawned dozens of touring companies that took it to audiences all over Britain and Ireland, raking in millions.

One person who saw it was a vacationing American businessman named Horace Liveright. He'd made his name in publishing, drawing praise for his fight against censorship and his "discovering" talents like Ernest Hemingway, William Faulkner, Hart Crane, Dorothy Parker and S. J. Perelman. He was also heavily criticized, particularly in England, for what some—especially those in the privileged classes—considered overly aggressive marketing of his novels.

He knew the play would be a huge hit in New York if he made some minor changes. The Americanization process began when he hired a young journalist named John Balderston to transform Deane's stilted, almost Elizabethan dialogue into conversational English, and cut the lame scenes in which Dracula actually hisses at the audience. He decided to keep, however, the high-collared cape Dracula wore (Deane used his own in London) as a bit of Old World flair.

He made one other change, too. Dissatisfied with Huntley's frumpy portrayal of the count, Liveright scoured the New York theater scene for someone who could add charm, mystery and gravity to the role. He found him in a little play called *The Red Poppy*. One of the supporting characters was played by a tall, handsome man with great stage presence, a thick accent and a very distinctive way of delivering his lines. The actor's unique enunciation came from the fact that he spoke English very poorly and had learned his lines phonetically.

As a young man in Lugos, Hungary (now Lugoj, Romania), tall Bela Blasko used his good looks and charm to win a number of roles on stage and in Hungarian silent films. After serving as an infantry lieutenant in the Austro-Hungarian army in World War I, he returned to find that the political atmosphere at home had changed and decided to leave for his own safety.

He fled to Germany and eventually the United States. A bit of confusion at Ellis Island led to his last name being changed from Blasko to Lugosi (Hungarian for "the man from Lugos"). He was surprised to find a large and vibrant Hungarian community in New York City and soon found work in Hungarian-language theater. Ambitious and realizing that the real money came from English-speaking productions, he did his best to learn the language and took small, often non-speaking roles, whenever he could.

As soon as Liveright hired him for *Dracula*, Lugosi made the role his own. Even in rehearsals, he would often draw applause for his creepy, but compelling performances.

Opening in 1931, *Dracula* was a smash hit, both critically and commercially. Lugosi, whose English had by then improved considerably, became a star almost overnight. He took the role to heart—often wearing his costume out on the town after shows—and was considered a major heartthrob.

Talkies had just been introduced and Hollywood was desperate for dialogue-heavy scripts. A minor bidding war erupted for Balderston's version of *Dracula* and Universal, headed by Carl Laemme Jr., won. Laemme Jr. loved the play, the script, everything except Lugosi. While he admitted stage audiences were enthralled by him, he felt that his accent and overall strangeness would be off-putting to most Americans.

Instead, he would cast Lon Chaney—with whom he had worked on *The Hunchback of Notre Dame* and *The Phantom of the Opera*—in the title role. Lugosi didn't give up and hung around the production, helping where he could. He even traveled to England to negotiate a deal for the motion picture rights with Florence, bringing her asking price down from $60,000 to $40,000. But Laemme wouldn't budge, refusing to offer Lugosi even a bit part.

Just before filming was to begin, Chaney died of cancer. Desperate, Laemme offered the part to the role of Count Dracula to John Wray, Paul Muni, Conrad Veidt, Chester Morris and William Courtenay—well-known leading men of the time—but none were interested. Finally, he offered the role to Lugosi, but cut the film's budget in half and paid him the insultingly tiny wage—even for the era—of just $3500.

It was a huge risk—a horror film with no comedy relief, no trick ending and an eccentric star whose command of the English language was iffy at best. And it was a risk that paid off handsomely. As soon as it was released on Valentine's Day 1931, audiences flocked to *Dracula*. When the national media began to report that women were fainting in their seats at screenings, people swarmed theaters out of curiosity.

Lugosi was the key. People loved him, especially women. After *Dracula*, Lugosi actually received more fan mail and even marriage proposals than reigning superstars Clark Gable and Errol Flynn.

But Lugosi (who once said his greatest thrill was a "paycheck") squandered his fame by taking any role, no matter how bad, and by becoming addicted to drugs. With his physical and mental health steadily declining, Lugosi became an increasingly ridiculous figure as he pulled out the old "wampire" shtick for anyone who would pay him.

While most people these days remember his self-parody better than his original claim to fame, Lugosi had made his mark on cinematic history. He established the romantic, erotic allure of the vampire in the Western consciousness.

But while Florence Stoker was diligent in her defense of her late husband's copyright, she was eventually made powerless in the United States. Apparently, Stoker's representatives didn't completely understand the then-complicated process of U.S. copyright and *Dracula* was never actually registered as her property there.

This led to a deluge of poorly made, poorly received, cliché-ridden versions of the story, bringing its cultural currency to the same level as Lugosi's career. And Lugosi—pulling out the cape for a steadily declining level of comedy TV shows and state fairs—who was getting more pathetic and disturbing rather than scary and romantic with every passing year, certainly didn't help.

The story could have died of its own tattered legacy had it not been for two major efforts. In 1958, Hammer Films (a British company and thus subject to copyright) released a new version of *Dracula*. Powered by the highly charged performance of Christopher Lee as Dracula, this version was a minor hit and allowed Hammer to make a series of low-budget, high-return horror films for decades. It was retitled *The Horror of Dracula* for U.S. audiences because the immensely popular 1931 version was still showing in a few theaters around the country.

The story was revived successfully again in 1977 when the play re-opened on Broadway. It was a big success, with towering, broodingly handsome Frank Langella redefining the character for another generation of theater-goers. Langella then starred in a big-budget film adaptation in 1979. It was soundly praised—especially Langella's performance—but wasn't very successful at the box office, in large part because director John Badham was subtle and sparing in the film's violent scenes and because the silly but much-hyped vampire-based spoof *Love At First Bite* was released on the same day.

As effective as Lee and Langella were, they failed to capture a mass audience, especially among young people, the way Lugosi had. But vampires made yet another, even bigger comeback.

In the very late 1970s, punk rock had clearly run its course. In its wake, a variety of more complex musical styles—known collectively as post-punk—emerged. A group of bands, many of them veteran punk outfits like The Cure and Siouxsie and the Banshees, began to diversify and started performing songs about existentialist philosophy, romanticism and even gothic horror. They also developed a common look—black often anachronistic clothes, black hair and heavy makeup.

Typical of these bands was Bauhaus. Originally a melodic punk outfit who performed in jeans and T-shirts, the members of Bauhaus sensed which way the wind was blowing, changed into an all-black uniform and released their first single in 1980: "Bela Lugosi's Dead."

Lugosi—or at least his 1931 portrayal of *Dracula*—quickly became iconic to this rapidly emerging subculture. As the music became more and more dreary, the people listening to it manifested their feelings of eroticism and romance by dressing in increasingly more elaborate ways, often imitating the styles of Lugosi's Dracula or similar clichés taken from German Expressionist horror or Alice Cooper's act—but always in variations recalling *Dracula*.

The fans, already being called Goths by their peers, needed a Mecca. They got it in July 1982 when Olli Wisdom, the founder of a glam-turned-Goth band called Specimen, opened the Batcave in London's trendy Soho district. A live-music venue and nightclub, the Batcave's house band was Specimen, but established bands like The Cure, Siouxsie and the Banshees, and Bauhaus played there frequently, as did newer acts like Alien Sex Fiend, Sisters of Mercy, and Dead Can Dance.

The club's decor was nearly totally dark and dominated by fake cobwebs, rubber bats and other items reminiscent of Dracula's castle. In a back room, gothic horror films—including, reportedly, illegal prints of both *Dracula* and *Nosferatu*—played constantly.

Just as the Goth movement was beginning to gain a little traction, they got a vampire movie to call their own. Tony Scott, a talented British commercial and music video director, lived in the shadow of his older brother Ridley, who became world-famous after directing the blockbuster *Alien* in 1979. Eventually, interest in Ridley became interest in Tony, because they had worked together for years.

When Hollywood came calling, Tony was ready. He had read Anne Rice's 1976 novel *Interview With the Vampire* earlier that year and thought it would make a splendid film. MGM, which already had Rice's novel in development, had a different idea. They thought Tony's fast-paced style would be better suited to a more modern, less clichéd take on vampires. William Strieber's 1980 novel *The Hunger* was little known, but much loved by a small army of fans. It was groundbreaking for the genre because it dealt very frankly and pragmatically with the mundanity of vampire life—finding suitable victims, disposing of bodies—while retaining the gothic necessities of horror, romance and eroticism. Streiber worked hard to make the vampires in his novel sympathetic characters. They were actually the real victims, born into (or at least seduced by) a lifestyle that made them different from a mainstream culture that could never begin to understand them.

With *The Hunger*, Tony Scott made a vampire epic. By combining a trio of popular young actors (David Bowie, Catherine Deneuve and Susan Sarandon), sumptuous design, haute couture fashion and a cutting-edge soundtrack (including Bauhaus's "Bela Lugosi's Dead"), Scott created a *Dracula* for a new age. While *The Hunger*—a lavish movie released at a time when stark, spartan filmmaking was fashionable—didn't set any records at the box office and wasn't a critical success, it was considered required viewing by Goths. Because of their dedication, *The Hunger* was kept alive in theaters for years as a second-run film, drawing audiences (often in costume) for midnight showings.

And their numbers were growing. The look was easy to copy and nearly identical-looking herds of Goths—sometimes called batcavers because of the London nightclub—were commonplace in high schools throughout Europe, North America and Australia by the middle 1980s.

The numbers of Goths have risen and fallen, but, as a group, they have had staying power. Decades after kids started dressing up in black, they're still doing it. It's a testament to the movement that other fashion trends that came out of the same milieu—like New Romantics or Modern Primitives—have essentially died out.

* * *

There's a strong reason for Goth's longevity. Traditionally, the Goth crowd has attracted the least popular kids, those who are most alienated and fit in the worst. They are generally those who don't succeed athletically, academically or in other social circles.

An extensive study in Scotland published in the *British Medical Journal* in 2004 indicated that teenagers who identified themselves as Goths were more than twice as likely as other teens to self-harm and to entertain suicidal thoughts. Interestingly, in almost every case, the child in question showed a greater propensity for these and other signs of depression, *before* they identified themselves as Goths. It's as if the Goths attracted the most depressed kids in the community and eased their angst a little.

For many of these alienated, unpopular kids, inclusion into the Goth subculture can be a godsend. Goths tend to be very welcoming of new recruits and offer a more-or-less supportive community for those who don't already have one.

I ran this by three Goths who agreed to talk with me at a Queen Street coffee shop. Swansong, a tall, thin guy of about 30, was squiring around two women about 10 years his junior. Hellwind is short and stocky, while Ravenesque is short and obese. In a subculture—or at least a fashion statement—based on eroticism, almost all of the Goths I've met do not exactly present as the current mainstream ideal of sleek and sexy.

These three are all wearing nothing but black and white, though other Goths around also experiment with dark purple and, occasionally, blood red.

Swansong admits that the established hypothesis was true for him. "I had no friends, none at all, not even in my family," he said. "Then I started hanging around with the Goths at my school, dressing like them, and I had dozens of friends . . . all ages . . . girls too . . . even if they mostly didn't go to my school." And his new appearance served as an entree into a larger world. "I went on a trip [to a distant town] with my parents and ran into some Goth kids in the parking lot of a grocery store, and we immediately started talking, hanging out—that never would have happened if I weren't a Goth."

Like that other successful fashion movement from the same era, punk (which was initially conceived in Sex Pistols' manager Malcolm McLaren's

London boutique), the Goth look is designed as much to anger those outside the movement as it is to please those within it. "People notice me now," he says. "They don't all like me, but they never would have anyway—this way, at least, I get a reaction."

Swansong says he has lots of pleasant (or at least fulfilling) memories of being a Goth, but adds that the consensus in his community is that the golden days of Goth are long over. Two things, he said, have combined to keep Goths away from the clubs: the Internet and the murders. "The murders especially," pipes in Hellwind. "They blame them on us because we're different."

The Internet is a problem, they explain to me, because Goths are generally shy people who are difficult to coax out of their shells, not to mention their homes. And it's a lot easier for them to make friends semi-anonymously on forums and in chat rooms than it is to actually go out into clubs and face the possible disaster of rejection. Since Goths recruit from those who already feel rejected from mainstream society, not fitting in at a Goth club would be a profound disappointment. It's hard to imagine how bad it would feel to be rejected by a group of people who got together because they all felt rejected.

Hellwind points out that all the clubs serve alcohol, which means those under 19 aren't permitted. "And they're way more strict about it these days," she says. "When I was young, it was no problem getting into clubs—now they card everyone who looks under 30."

I take a quick scan around the Goths in the neighborhood and notice that the median age appears to be around 30, maybe higher. I ask about this and my tablemates tell me that there are lots of young Goths, but they're at home typing away, not coming out to clubs. Making matters worse, the people at the clubs generally feel disdain for the younger, plugged-in Goths.

"They're not real Goths," Swansong says, but in our conversation, he has said the same thing about basically every person or group mentioned except those at our table. "And the Internet, it makes them crazy . . . violent."

The perception that Goths were violent first emerged in 1999 after the Columbine High School massacre, when two teenagers killed 12 fellow students, a teacher and themselves. After the media found that one of the participants had dyed black hair and wore eye makeup in a ninth-grade yearbook photo, the killers were widely described as Goths. Even Diane Sawyer dropped the G-word on national TV.

Although the connection between the Columbine killers and the Goth culture was never decisively proven and is still widely disputed, the link in the public consciousness was made. For better or worse, and true or not, Goths became associated with hateful nerds, ready to lash out at those who had made fun of them in the past. Perhaps making matters worse, Marilyn Manson (a band associated with Goth culture, although rarely by Goths themselves) cancelled three dates in memoriam for the Columbine victims. That sealed it for many.

Of course, other Goths found the link between the Columbine killers and their subculture ridiculous. "Goth is about being beautiful," Lance Goth (real name: Andrew Lee), then-owner of Sanctuary, told Toronto's *Now* magazine. "Maybe you're mourning your existence or the way humanity is, but that doesn't make you want to get an AK-47 and kill people."

It didn't matter; Goths were already identified in the public consciousness as potential killers. After Columbine, the media sought a Goth angle for pretty well every teen crime with varying levels of success. It became routine: a) kid kills, b) media looks in his bedroom and finds some black hair dye, c) media calls him a Goth, d) media interviews local Goths who invariably deny the kid was ever a Goth.

A perfect example came in the person of Kimveer Gill. Large-scale media and public scrutiny was directed at the Goths again in 2006 when Gill, a self-described Goth, went to Montreal's Dawson College and shot the place up. Despite constantly practicing his shooting for years, Gill proved to have poor aim, firing hundreds of shots that killed one person and injured twenty more before he took his own life after a police officer managed to shoot him in the left arm.

Unlike Eric Harris and Dylan Klebold, the perpetrators of the Columbine massacre, Gill left the media an easy-to-follow trail of his beliefs, ideas and self-image.

VampireFreaks.com is an online community for Goths. Users can create profiles, post photos of and information about themselves, and be rated by other members. Started in 1999 as the offshoot of the personal webpage of Brooklyn-based industrial/Goth DJ Jet (real name: Jethro Berelman), VampireFreaks.com became instantly popular, as it was the only easily accessible Goth forum online. Now it has over a million users and a number of interest groups (called "cults"). VampireFreaks also releases music CDs of member-artists and sells apparel and other paraphernalia through another offshoot, fuckthemainstream.com.

But the mainstream didn't really notice any of this until Gill started shooting people. When an enterprising Montreal reporter found Gill's profile on VampireFreaks.com, images lifted from the site of Gill posing with a huge knife and pointing his many guns at the camera were transmitted worldwide. And so were the words he used to describe himself:

> His name is Trench. You will come to know him as the Angel of Death. He is male. He is 25 years of age. He lives in Quebec. He finds that it is an O.K place to live. He is not a people person. He has met a handful of people in his life who are decent. But he finds the vast majority to be worthless, no good, kniving [sic], betraying, lying, deceptive, motherfuckers..Work sucks . . . School sucks . . . Life sucks . . . What else can I say. Metal and Goth kick ass. Life is like a video game, you gotta die sometime. I hate this world, I hate the people in it, I hate the way people live, I hate God, I hate the deceivers, I hate betrayers, I hate religious zealots, I hate everything . . . I hate so much . . . (I could write 1,000 more lines like these, but does it really matter, does anyone even care) . . .

The word Goth stood out and the media started combing the world for an expert on the subject. They needed one quickly and they found him in Mick Mercer. Frequently described as a respected journalist and author of three books, Mercer was more than happy to comment. He gave the Associated Press his opinion of Gill:

> Not a Goth. Never a Goth. The bands he listed as his chosen form of ear-bashing were relentlessly Metal and standard Grunge, Rock and Goth Metal, with some Industrial presence. He had nothing whatsoever to do with Goth.

While Mercer's opinion became gospel because of the AP quote, something about the stridency of his denial and the pretentiousness of his choice of words seemed specious to me. So I looked up Mick Mercer. He's a Goth himself and has never written for a widely read or much-recognized publication. His three books on the Goth culture are self-serving and slow-selling. His self-published magazine—which he calls *The Mick*—is mostly about his travels and his cats. It's free and has no advertisers, but contains many requests for donations. His credentials as an impartial, qualified commentator are iffy at best.

And Gill himself would have disagreed with Mercer, perhaps violently. Not only did Gill describe himself as a "Goth" frequently, but he listed among his likes: Goth everything, www.VampireFreaks.com, black clothes, black everything, night, darkness, blood, *The Crow*, ravens, the Grim Reaper, horror movies, demons, Gothic artwork and other dark artwork. Among his dislikes, he listed: normal people, anyone who has anything against Metal or Goth, anyone who has ever said or done anything bad to a Goth girl, and sunlight.

While it could be argued endlessly and pointlessly whether Gill was a Goth or not (though he clearly and frequently identified himself as such), the matter is academic now. Once the media identified him as a Goth and had his VampireFreaks.com profile to back it up, people began fearing Goths as ticking time bombs, ready to take revenge on those who had forced them to be Goths.

Jet responded with a press release that said (in part): "Just because someone goes around shooting people and happens to be a member of VampireFreaks, doesn't mean that this website has influenced him to do such a horrible thing." He pointed out that just four murders had been linked to the site, which then had 606,000 members. That was a lower homicide rate than the one in the mainstream community, he noted.

Of course, most people found that reasoning specious. Parry Aftab is a lawyer specializing in Web-related crime and security issues and the executive director of Wired Safety, an organization that monitors potentially dangerous websites. VampireFreaks is one of the sites her group looks at most closely, and she claims the group's members are a lot more criminal that Jet allows. "We've had lots of problems with VampireFreaks," she said. "We're finding many of the kids who are highly troubled and those who are making trouble for others are gravitating to that site."

The problem, as she sees it, is that when people collect in sites like these, it tends to "normalize aberrant behavior." While people might be reluctant to share their opinion in person, they are often emboldened to do so when surrounded by others who they perceive as like-minded.

I've experienced this phenomenon myself. I grew up as a fan of a certain American football team. Since they rarely won and were located in a small market far away from where I lived, I was the only fan of theirs I ever knew about. It was a situation very much like many Goths faced—I had an interest that was important to me and nobody to share it with. But once I got on the Internet, I found dozens of forums devoted to the team and spent many hours talking with my new friends from places as far away as Hawaii, Barcelona and Singapore about our common interest.

And there are forums and chat rooms devoted to everything now, from bird watching to child molesting. The theory—supported by many psychologists I spoke with—is that when people talk with others who share their opinion, it reinforces their opinion as correct. When someone has an interest that's outside the societal norm (or even against the law)—like dog fighting, for instance—they can find like-minded individuals to share their stories and opinions with. And, if you subscribe to the theory, they will be encouraged in their interest and reinforced that it's an acceptable one to have, in spite of the laws and popular scorn. The theory has been used repeatedly in the pursuit of evidence to use against Internet-based child pornography collectors.

And there is competition for attention among the online communities. "I think the site is starting to breed a different [kind of] Goth," Aftab said. "Some of these kids who are troubled know they'll only get attention on there if they do something different than everyone else—you have to up the ante." My own experiences on VampireFreaks.com have shown this to be true, as I have seen many members appear to try to be sexier or more gruesome than the rest.

Media scrutiny of VampireFreaks.com hasn't been limited to Canada, although both Jet and Aftab agree that the site is more popular with Canadians than any other nation. In the first part of the twenty-first century, murders and other crimes committed by teenagers identified as Goths or associated with the Goth lifestyle have made front pages in places as widely separated as England, Kansas and Australia.

In early 2006, a 23-year-old Long Island man, Eric Fischer, was charged with rape when a 13-year-old girl he had sex with went to police. Fischer later admitted using VampireFreaks.com to meet young girls. He'd arrange to meet them in a local cemetery after dark and then attempt to have sex with them.

The site made front pages again later in 2006 when the bodies of a husband, wife and young son were found in Medicine Hat, Alberta. The prime suspect was the 12-year-old daughter of the family.

She was arrested the following day not far away, in Leader, Saskatchewan, with her boyfriend, 23-year-old Jeremy Allen Steinke.

After the arrest, the story unraveled. Though it has been frequently reported that the couple met on VampireFreaks.com, this may not be true. They both had accounts at the site. His stated a fondness for "blood, razor blades and pain," while hers listed "hatchets, serial killers and blood" as her interests. But a close friend of hers attests that she actually saw them meet at a concert in Medicine Hat.

After their initial meeting, they communicated mainly via Nexopia.com, another social-networking website popular with young people in Western Canada. She lied about her age—Nexopia.com requires that users be at least 15 years old—and called herself "runawaydevil." To introduce people to her profile page, she wrote: "welcome to my tragic end."

After the parents found out about their daughter's relationship with Steinke, they grounded her and forbade her to see her boyfriend. A few days later, they and their young son were murdered, and their daughter and Steinke were on the run.

But before they left Medicine Hat, the runaway couple stopped by the apartment of a friend. He also had an account on VampireFreaks.com, but no definitive link was ever established between him and the suspects on the site by local law enforcement. The friend claimed to be a 300-year-old werewolf and performed a "marriage ceremony" that he claimed would unite the couple throughout eternity. Then they ran and, not surprisingly, were caught right away.

The daughter is the youngest person ever convicted of multiple murder in Canada. She received the maximum penalty for an offender under 14 years old—ten years—which will include four years in a psychiatric institution. Steinke has yet to be tried.

As was the drill, a reporter from the *Edmonton Journal* asked a local Goth what she thought of the media coverage. "Now I don't know about any one else," she responded, "but I'm completely outraged by the information they actually printed in this article, it hints at every single person fitting this 'description' to be a murderous blood-fending [sic] vampire."

I found that a strange opinion—that a free media should be censured for reporting pertinent facts regarding a murder suspect because it could bias the public against a group she considered herself part of. I wondered if she would hold the same opinion if the suspect were, say, a football player or a collector of true-crime books.

Swansong and his friends agree with her, though. "As Goths, we have to put up with a lot of bullshit," he says. "We're already labeled enough things, we don't need to be called murderers too."

After a long pause, Hellwind agrees. "Murders happen all the time, but when a Goth murders someone, it makes the front page." I ask her why she thinks that's the case. "Because people want to be able to identify a bad person," she answers. "People want to be able to point at anyone who's not normal and say 'I know you're bad.'"

I asked them if they'd had any problems because of the media portrayals of Goths. "We get so much abuse on a day-to-day basis, it's hard to tell where people's prejudices come from," Swansong says.

"But I noticed people became especially nasty after what happened to little Johnathon," Hellwind adds.

"He was no Goth," Swansong snapped, referring not to the victim or the killer, but his accomplice, Timothy Ferriman. "He was a vampire."

I immediately say the most wrong thing possible: "I thought you all dressed up like vampires."

They think that's an absurd statement and go into long colloquies about what Goth really is and isn't. Most of it is self-praise, but it boils down to one main distinction: Goth is a dress-up routine, but there are really people out there who consider themselves actually to be vampires.

I ask if they can introduce me to some. Again, they can't believe how stupid I am. "Goths and vampires rarely mix," says Hellwind angrily.

Okay, I say, can they point some out? They take me outside and show me a couple of guys milling about. They look kind of Goth-y but without the makeup and with more leather—floor-length coats and almost knee-high boots. They look very much like the very best interpretation of Victorian-era noblemen as filtered through K-Mart. The main difference between the two of them is that one has long hair and one has short hair.

I introduce myself and tell them what I'm doing. At first they decline to speak to me because they believe that the "mainstream" media distorts everything about them. But I can tell it's just an act, that these guys badly want the attention, and I tell them they can meet me in the coffee shop, if they change their minds.

When they show up, the Goths leave. The vampires sit with me and refuse to give their real names. One claims I couldn't pronounce his real name anyway. They seem so touchy, so on edge, that I don't argue. They assert that they are vampires, and not just pretend ones like the rest of the people I've been talking to.

I ask them if they drink blood. They both say they do—that is, after all, what makes them vampires. They tell me that they call blood by its proper name, "spiritus." One of them then informs me that's the Latin word for blood.

I have to restrain myself from them telling it isn't—"spiritus" means breathing in Latin, "sanguineus" means blood—because their self-burnished veneer of intellect seems so very important to them.

Instead, I ask them where they get it. They demur until one says that he can usually convince one of his "lovers" to cut themselves for him. This makes some sense. As noted by the British study mentioned earlier, many Goths and their associates practice self-harm, including cutting themselves. Self-cutting is normally associated with adolescents, usually girls, and can be an indicator of low self-esteem and/or pathological perfectionism. Convincing a self-cutter to contribute their blood doesn't seem like a very difficult task.

He then shows me his weapon of choice and I'm a little bit disappointed that it's not fangs. Inside the small sterilized foil packets he hands me are lancets—tiny blades intended for diabetics to use to draw blood for samples. "They're quick, clean and almost painless," he tells me.

Then comes the hard question—*why?*

"You wouldn't understand," they both answer simultaneously.

I ask them to try me.

"Well, there's a spirit to it—that's why the Romans called it 'spiritus' and we do too—it adds something to your . . . your . . . spirit that you can't get otherwise," the long-haired one said. "It's a spiritual thing—you wouldn't understand—we know we're vampires and our destiny is to drink blood."

In their defense, blood is pretty nutritious. It has plenty of protein and, obviously, iron. Those facts are known to many cultures and cooking with blood is not uncommon in many parts of the world. Blood pudding (also called black pudding) is commonplace throughout much of Europe, including the British Isles. The Masai and other East African peoples frequently drink their cattle's blood. I remember eating at a Vietnamese restaurant when my wife ordered the rare beef soup. The helpful waiter asked her if she wanted the blood "in the soup or on the side."

But that's animal blood, which is normally prepared and served in a hygienic manner like any other animal product. Drinking human blood, on the other hand, is an easy way to transmit disease. I called the U.S. Centers for Disease Control in Atlanta and told a doctor there I was planning on drinking human blood. After she suggested I see a psychiatrist, the doctor I spoke with told me that I should be inoculated against cholera, influenza, filariasis, anthrax, typhus, leptospirosis, lyme disease, malaria, meningitis, black plague, tuberculosis, intestinal worms, rabies, typhoid fever and yellow fever—just in case. She also told me I was taking my chances with HIV/AIDS and that there are "plenty of other ways to have a good time."

But these self-described vampires aren't interested in nutrition and only obliquely concerned about safety. They drink blood, not as a foodstuff, but as a sacrament. And they are quick to point out that Christians do the same thing (at least symbolically) through the sacrament of Communion. They are convinced that drinking human blood heightens their spirituality, just as warriors from many different cultures ritualistically ate various body parts of their enemies to give them strength. They believe this, it would appear, because they so very much want it to be true.

But they tell me that their spirituality doesn't extend towards awakening the dead, super-long life spans, shape changing or near invincibility, when I bring them up. "That's all typical Hollywood bullshit," the longhaired one tells me. Again he's wrong. Those attributes are actually essential parts of the original vampire myths; the only parts added by the film industry are the wardrobes, which these guys ape obsessively. "Vampires aren't monsters with magic powers," the shorthaired one tells me. "Just people with a different belief system."

I ask them about Ferriman. "He was no vampire!" the shorthaired one shouts. "He was a total wannabe! A poseur!" His friend echoes his sentiments just as angrily. After they calm down, I ask them what made him a fake, in essence. What made them real vampires and him not. They speak obliquely about lifestyle and spirituality, but give me nothing concrete. So I ask them, what makes a vampire a vampire, then, is it drinking blood? They seem confused. They say that was part of it, a big part of it. I tell them that I have independently corroborated evidence that Ferriman drank blood.

Exasperated, the longhaired one sighs and throws his hands in the air. He looks at his pal and said: "Let's get out of here." They mutter a few things about how horrible the mainstream media is, threaten to sue me (though I have no idea why) and take off.

After those initial encounters, I've spoken to dozens of Goths and vampires, some in person, some online. A few commonalities arose. All of the Goths I met said they were shy people, but all considered themselves extremely intelligent, just misunderstood. All of them liked to cultivate an air of erudition, frequently using arcane words and unnecessessarily complicated syntax and thought processes, along with a liberal dose of what they considered philosophy, in conversation. As I expected, most of them generally became Goths less because of a fascination with things dark and dreary (few even knew who Bela Lugosi was, let alone idolized him), but because they were shut out by or not interested in other social circles at school. They were all adept at rationalizing things to support each of their opinions (no matter how illogical) and were quick to become angry or withdraw if that opinion was challenged or even questioned. And all of them took at least some time out to deny the Goth qualifications of somebody, often a friend.

But that's about as far as the malice usually went with the Goths. There are, of course, good and bad people in every group; but Goths generally seemed to want to avoid confrontation, even fear it. And they seemed less likely to hurt others than themselves. I talked to a cop I know from Hamilton, Ontario, about Goths, and he agreed. "I see Goths all the time—but only as victims," he said. "If a Goth were gonna commit a crime, other than suicide, I'd expect it to be something sneaky and anonymous—like arson or something."

Vampires, on the other hand, seemed to be all about malevolence. And, I think, they would be pleased to know that I think so. There is, in my experience, a very distinct difference between dressing up like a vampire and actually believing you are one.

Although there's no real vampire organization, there is a group called the Temple, which acts as such in a *de facto* manner. Situated in the extraordinarily boring, predominantly white suburb-of-a-suburb of Lacey, Washington, the Temple claims to speak for all vampires. Open up their website, and you will be treated to their motto: "Vampire, the traditional name given to those at the top of the food chain." And if you dig deeper, you can read the vampire creed:

> I am a Vampire.
>
> I worship my ego and I worship my life, for I am the only God that is.
>
> I am proud that I am a predatory animal and I honor my animal instincts.
>
> I exalt my rational mind and hold no belief that is in defiance of reason.
>
> I recognize the difference between the worlds of truth and fantasy.
>
> I acknowledge the fact that survival is the highest law.
>
> I acknowledge the Powers of Darkness to be hidden natural laws through which I work my magic.
>
> I know that my beliefs in Ritual are fantasy but the magic is real,
>
> And I respect and acknowledge the results of my magic.
>
> I realize there is no heaven as there is no hell,
>
> And I view death as the destroyer of life.
>
> Therefore I will make the most of life here and now.
>
> I am a Vampire.
>
> Bow down before me.

I remembered all of this in the coffee shop after the Toronto vampires left me, so I paid the check and followed them outside because I wanted to ask them about what they thought of the vampire's creed.

It occurred to me then that the whole vampire thing is a way to adopt a feeling of superiority over others. But these guys, these vampires—there was nothing superior about them at all. They were of average intellect (despite what they believed), not particularly handsome or engaging or charismatic. Neither had accomplished anything of import in their lives; they had nothing, aside from their status as vampires, to be proud of.

I realized, while I was walking down Queen Street West after them, that the whole vampire thing is nothing more than an elaborate scam. It's a way for people who are so downtrodden in real life to have a pretend world where everybody "bows down" to them. The only problem is that some people take it too seriously. And nobody actually bows.

I want to catch up to the vampires I met—these role models for Tim Ferriman; they were living the life he pretended to, he really wanted to be just like them—to see what they think about my hypothesis. I'm interested to see what their rebuttal is. But they have a few blocks' head start on me. So I start to run. I finally catch up to them about three blocks away. I've been jogging a bit, so I'm a bit out of breath when I tap the shoulder of the long-haired one. As I take a moment to catch my breath, I look into their faces and see abject terror.

The long-haired one runs away—he just flees. I look at the short-haired one and I can see that he's actually weeping. And I don't mean that there is a stoic tear emerging from his eyes: this guy is bawling. I'm a big guy, but not really intimidating in the normal world and I certainly didn't intend to frighten these guys. But I literally have to hug the guy to calm him down enough to talk. "We didn't mean to piss you off, man," he says to me. "We'll talk to you if you want."

It's okay, I tell him. I have everything I need.

CHAPTER 4

# kevin's a very troubled boy

It was meant to be a nice, heartwarming bit of holiday cheer, but the effect, seen now, is starkly the opposite. On December 22, 2002, a local Toronto news station, Citytv, aired a video news report—just about a minute and a half long—of firefighters coming to the aid of an unfortunate east end family. The Champagnies, at 90 Dawes Road, had suffered a terrible fire just four days earlier.

The firefighters had it out in 20 minutes and nobody was hurt, but the house was gutted. The family's Christmas gifts and preparations were destroyed and they were living in a temporary apartment.

The video opens with a shot of Ralston Champagnie surrounded by burned wires uprooted from the pale green walls. There are patches of exposed drywall and wood; and there appears to be nothing in the house except for the people talking. Ralston nods and agrees with the reporter's unheard assertion that the fire was "devastating."

The scene cuts to a fire engine rolling down a city street with its siren on. The reporter says: "Call it déjà vu. Last week the Champagnie family watched from the front lawn as fire trucks raced down their street. Today, they watch the same scene—but for a very different reason."

The fire engine stops. A pair of firefighters step out, each with a large clear plastic bag full of parcels. The bags are handed to the

Champagnies' two sons, Kevin Madden and Johnathon Madden. You can't really see what Kevin got, but Johnathon received a slot-car racetrack and an NCAA basketball, among other things.

The boys are standing in the yard in front of 90 Dawes with their bags. It's cold out and neither boy is wearing a hat. Kevin's cheeks are bright red, in stark contrast to the rest of his pasty complexion. He's grinning, maybe smirking. Johnathon stands beside his brother, the top of his head below the level of Kevin's armpits. His head is down and he refuses to face the camera. Some people I've shown the video to say he looks scared, others say embarrassed.

The action then cuts to Ralston and his wife Joanne shaking hands with a senior firefighter. All three are wearing black leather jackets and both men have shaved heads. The camera then focuses on the senior firefighter, although the text on the screen misidentifies him as "Rolstan Champagnie: Fire victim," misspelling Ralston's first name. He talks about how "horrifying" it is for firefighters to see families like the Champagnies "out on the street" over the holidays.

The scene switches back to the front lawn, where a firefighter officially hands the bags to the boys. The firefighter passes the bag to Kevin and shakes his hand. The man is about an inch shorter than the boy and much slighter, despite his bulky uniform. The two avoid eye contact.

Back inside the house, the camera focuses on the twisted wires and burned-out electrical fixtures, then follows the pretty young reporter—Anne-Marie Green—to the bottom of a staircase, where she interviews Kevin. He towers above her and begins to recount how he found out the house was on fire:

> I was watching TV. I said, "Do you smell anything?" [A family member who can not be identified] says "no." Something's burning. She runs upstairs, she comes back downstairs: "Kevin, the house is on fire."

Throughout his story, Kevin is smiling, almost laughing. He's clearly having a great time. Still, he avoids looking at either the camera or the reporter. His eyes, instead, dart around the fringes of the room.

The scene switches to Ralston, who describes the fire as "the worst 20 minutes of my life" and maintains that his primary concern was for his family because he didn't know where they all were at the time.

Back outside, the video shows the firefighters handing the kids the bags again. "Thanks to the firefighters, the children received more presents than they would have on Christmas Day," Green's voice says pompously over the image. "And the entire family is extremely grateful."

The video cuts to Ralston, who repeatedly praises the people of Toronto, which he calls the "greatest city in the world." He calls his fellow Torontonians "open, honest, kind and giving."

The firefighters make one last pass in front of the lined-up family and the camera captures a brief glimpse of Johnathon's face. He flashes Kevin a broad grin and it's unclear of whether his brother sees him or not. To me, his smile doesn't indicate joy at receiving the gifts or being remembered during a time of family hardship. Instead, it appears to betray a kind of silliness, as though he finds the proceedings quite funny.

Another firefighter shakes hands with Kevin and again they don't look at each other's faces.

The video ends with Green dressed in faded jeans and a pullover "reporting live" from the Toronto Fire Department's station 332. It's not the station that responded to the fire — in fact, it's almost eight miles away and across the most-congested part of the city — but it is two blocks from Citytv's headquarters at Queen and John. Green, who now works in Philadelphia, closes with a comment about how investigators have determined that the fire was caused by faulty wiring, although two sources very close to the case believe that it may have begun after someone left a candle burning.

It's unnerving to see the tape now, knowing what I know. It's strange to see Johnathon, so shy, so tiny. But what's really disturbing is seeing Kevin. He's just so huge. A year before the murder, he was already massive and still growing. Significantly bigger than almost all of the adults in the video, he made Johnathon look almost like a toy in comparison.

And Kevin's attitude is strange. Although he never actually says anything blatantly inappropriate, his delight in the family's time of crisis seems strange, especially in retrospect.

* * *

Everyone who knew Kevin back then would describe him as strange, and many told me that he was at least a little nuts. He had sought or been strongly encouraged to seek psychological treatment on many occasions. So often, one medical professional told me, that most of the emergency room staff at one Toronto hospital knew him by sight.

At school, he was a regular in the principal's and guidance counselors' offices and—despite his school's tough reputation—feared in the halls and playground.

* * *

David (not his real name) comes into the coffee shop wearing the current uniform of disaffected youth in Toronto. Gone are the traditional jeans, leather jackets and tour shirts of a generation earlier. The rocker look has been replaced with something vaguely but not overtly hiphopish. As he saunters up to me, I can see that he's wearing oversized black jeans, a white t-shirt with a Fila logo and a black windbreaker, which I later see has "Perry Ellis" stitched on the back. He's also wearing a Boston Red Sox baseball cap. It's bright red, even though the Red Sox actually wear navy blue caps. David wears it set at a rakish angle, like a kid from the *Little Rascals*. What I really notice about the cap, though, is that the brim is perfectly straight—like it was adjusted with a ruler—rather than slightly curled, the way ball players actually wear them.

He plops down opposite me with a loud thud. Although he's almost painfully skinny, he stretches out to take up as much room as possible as though he is protecting the bench from someone trying to sit beside him. His baggy clothes help, but not much.

Up close I can see that his cheeks are ravaged by acne and that the hair on his head is only minutely longer than his patchy stubble.

We engage in a little small talk. I find out that he's graduated high school, but hasn't yet found any steady work. He makes a few bucks, he says, working with construction crews under the table, but doesn't like it because most of the guys don't speak English and working hard in very hot and very cold weather doesn't appeal to him. He's thinking of attending a local community college for HVAC—heating, ventilation and air conditioning maintenance—because "those guys have it made."

He lives with his mother. When he tells me this, he calls her his "moms," which immediately makes me think he's a member of a household headed by a lesbian couple, but when I put it in context of the rest of his faux-gangsta vocabulary, I realize it's just one woman.

When we begin to talk about Kevin, his speech becomes far less affected. There are fewer "yos" and his vowels shorten up. David doesn't claim to have been a great friend of Kevin's, just someone who hung around with the same people. And, if they were the only guys around, they sometimes hung out together. These social interactions usually centered around smoking. They didn't really do more than shoot the breeze most of the time, talking about girls, games, school and the regular stuff.

Kevin, he remembered, liked to laugh. He became especially animated when he was describing movies he'd seen, detailing the parts he thought were funny—usually when a character had been hurt or humiliated—laughing all the way. Conversely, David says, Kevin had very little tolerance for anyone else trying to be funny. "It's not that he thought he was the only funny guy," David says. "He just couldn't pay attention to what you had to say—he'd talk for a half hour and as soon as you'd open your mouth, he'd start up again . . . change the subject."

I asked him what else Kevin talked about and his answer was vague. I asked him if Kevin ever talked about his family. He told me "guys don't really talk about that kind of stuff," as though I came from a completely different culture. He does, however, recall that he knew Kevin had a little brother (whom he had never met) and that Kevin hated his stepfather. "Yeah, Kevin used to complain about him all the time," David says. "He thought he was a total asshole." David doesn't really give any more details. But he declares hatred for stepfathers to be commonplace in their community.

"He never mentioned his mother, though," he says. "Maybe he liked her."

I ask if Ralston's being black was a major problem for Kevin. I'd heard that Kevin had a problem with black people, and I wanted to see what his friend thought. David seems startled by the question. From his outfit and language, I could tell that David was apishly copying what he thought was black culture, and Kevin didn't dress much differently. David looked at me sheepishly and says: "I dunno."

I ask if he thought Kevin was a bully.

"It's hard to say," he tells me. "I mean, Kevin could be mean—smacking guys in the head or slamming them into lockers, but it's not like he picked on any one guy or one kind of guy; basically, anyone who was around might get the back of his hand." He thinks for a while. "Guy had mental problems," he says. "He wasn't a bully, just a mean guy . . . mean to just about everyone."

He recalls a few stories about Kevin that include him lashing out for no reason that David could discern and generally laughing it off if there was no obvious damage. He also noted that Kevin had a habit of making fun of anyone who had an obvious reaction to his assaults. "Yeah, if you yelled or made a big fuss, you were in trouble," David tells me. "Kevin would mock you . . . call you 'pussy' and laugh—you just kind of had to take it." He then nods and is quick to tell me that Kevin never bothered him that way, they were friends.

I ask David about retaliation, if any of the kids tried to get a little payback on Kevin after he hurt or humiliated them. He claims that there wasn't, but that another friend of theirs used to joke about some of the smaller guys getting angry enough to come back to school one day with a gun and "blow him away." Kevin didn't seem to take it seriously.

There is one story David tells me that seems to encapsulate Kevin's status as all-around tough guy. Kevin and a group of his peers were smoking and joking around in the park near their school. They were joined by a much larger group of kids and everybody was getting along, even if they were somewhat bored. One of the boys, Steve (not his real name), was chatting up a girl everyone knew he liked. They weren't actually dating, but everyone considered them to be *de facto* boyfriend and girlfriend, and it was obvious that Steve just didn't have enough confidence yet to ask her out. "So Kevin just goes up, walks up behind her and grabs both of her tits," David tells me. The girl, he says, was angry, but far from panicked. She glared at Kevin, called him an asshole and left. The other two girls who were there left with her. Kevin just laughed and made sucking noises.

"But Steve freaked out," David says. "He was yelling at Kevin, screaming, about what an asshole he was, what a shithead." Kevin was laughing at Steve's impotent rage and called him a "fag." Enraged and crying, Steve picked up a stick from the ground and threw it at Kevin. It hit him in the chest and bounced off. Kevin took a single step towards Steve. Obviously crying, Steve ran off, leaving his backpack behind. Kevin shouted "you better run, fag!" and started laughing. Before long, the rest of the guys were laughing at Steve as well.

"What about Steve?" I ask.

"Oh, he got over it," David tells me. "He was hanging around with Kevin again a week or so later."

"And nothing happened to Kevin?"

"Nothing EVER happened to Kevin."

* * *

While talking with a psychoanalyst who had a working knowledge of the case, I was getting nowhere getting him to explain what was wrong with Kevin Madden. The forensic scientist who had examined him at the Center for Addiction and Mental Health called him a "psychopath," so I asked the psychoanalyst to explain exactly what that meant.

"Well, most of us don't like to use terms like that anymore," he told me. Then he began to explain what it did mean, back when it was still in vogue. But the thing he told me that made the most impact was that, to understand how mental illness works, you have to see it in action. On his suggestion, I went looking for it at my children's school. Since he gave me a few tips on what this kind of mental illness looked like, it didn't take long to find.

"Jason threw a brick at Emily today," my seven-year-old son told me as I came up to greet him in the yard. (None of the kids' names are real.) He didn't seem scared or upset when he told me. It was more like he was reporting the mundane news of the day, like a surprise spelling test or some kid wetting his pants.

Although there are at least a dozen Jasons at the school, I immediately knew who he meant. I had first noticed him at a ball hockey game. While all the other kids who weren't playing were watching the game, Jason was constantly moving around the gym and making noise. He wasn't talking or singing or making funny noises to entertain the other boys; he was screaming, screaming as loudly and irritatingly as he could. It was all nonsense, seemingly designed to be annoying as possible. Instead of trying to make things better for those around him, he appeared bent on trying to ruin everyone else's good time.

The coach, a friend of mine, repeatedly asked him to stop. "Quiet, Jason," he said, over and over again. "Please be quiet, Jason." It didn't do any good. Eventually he gave up, but Jason didn't. He just kept on screaming. Both he and the coach knew there wasn't anything anyone could do about it.

When Jason finally got to play, he didn't help his team much. He spent most of his time on the floor swinging his stick at shoulder level and yelling at the other kids as they ran by. The coach diligently noted and corrected every other incidence of high sticking, but had already given up on Jason, who was pretty much allowed to do whatever he wanted.

When Jason was subbed out again, he came to sit beside me. He didn't like me, but he stared at me a lot. He kept his stick, even though another kid who was actually playing asked him if he could use it. He used it repeatedly to jab at the ball when it came near—showing far more alertness and coordination than he did while playing—and at players on both teams. While sitting out, he hit at least four kids with his stick. He denied two and claimed the other two were accidents. I was watching, he was lying on all four.

Then a kid I know, Miguel, a good kid, stepped over the bench to get off the floor. He tried to step over Jason, who was lying down in his way, but Miguel's foot grazed Jason's back. "You kicked me!' Jason shouted. "You kicked me!" He then made a sound that was sort of like crying, though there weren't any tears. Then he ran, still making that noise, all the way to the coach, and begged and pleaded with him to punish Miguel.

Jason was still complaining when his turn to play came up again. He started out trying hard, but quickly became distracted. The one time he managed to get his stick on the ball, my son managed to steal it from him. Immediately I was concerned. Jason and my son normally get along, but in his state of mind and with a potential weapon in his hand, I wasn't sure it'd be okay. It wasn't.

After the steal, Jason chased my son around the floor, swinging his stick at his head and missing. He never came close to connecting, mostly because he stopped to swing and my son (who had no idea this was going on behind him) never stopped moving.

Jason soon tired of this, or forgot why he was angry. Instead, he set up camp behind one of the nets and started moving it around. He wasn't trying to give his team any advantage; rather, he just seemed to enjoy upsetting the goalie. Eventually, a couple of bigger boys came over and stood on the back of the net so Jason couldn't move it anymore. He swore at them, then went to the center of the floor and swung his stick, oblivious to the game that was mercifully coming to an end around him.

After the game, I asked the coach about Jason. "Oh, he's a handful, all right," he said. "But he didn't hurt anybody—and he's just seven." To me, he seemed to be more than a handful. He appeared to be fixated on hurting someone, anyone other than himself. And, as the weeks and months passed, I found out later that he did hurt people. My son would tell me that Jason had kicked this kid or thrown something at another kid. I asked my son if Jason had ever done anything to him. He looked at me, astonished, and said, "No, I'm bigger than him." He then shook his head as though I had asked him something so stupid he was almost too embarrassed on my behalf to answer. I found out that a few run-ins with boys his size or larger didn't always end well for Jason, so he learned to target smaller, weaker or less bold children, usually girls.

Jason's parents won't talk to me, but their close neighbor (who has kids at the same school) offered her observations. "He's always been like that, even when he was a toddler," she told me. "My kids won't go near him, I don't have to tell them." She also told me that Jason's mom had told her that they were seeking help for Jason's Attention Deficit/Hyperactivity Disorder (better known as ADHD).

Said to affect about one in twenty people in the world, ADHD is a behavioral disorder indicated by a lack of attention, forgetfulness, distractibility and poor impulse control. That last symptom means that people with ADHD find it harder to control their desires when they come in conflict with social mores. For example, a child who shouts out answers in class, even though he or she knows the procedure is to raise his or her hand and wait to be acknowledged by the teacher, is showing poor impulse control.

Many people deny or minimize the existence of ADHD, suggesting that the symptoms that fit the profile really just amount to childish behavior and that we as a society are just too willing to rationalize, justify, classify and ultimately medicate any situation for the sake of convenience. ADHD was even parodied in *The Onion* as "youthful tendency disorder." But the medical community and millions of concerned parents are convinced that it's real.

Although the name ADHD is relatively new, the concept isn't. Hippocrates of Cos II, almost universally considered the father of modern medicine and the author of the famed Hippocratic Oath, wrote about a condition in 493 B.C. that we would now recognize as ADHD. He attributed the disorder to an excess of fire in the patient's bodily humors and prescribed lots of water and a bland diet that forbade red meat.

For a very long time after that, ADHD was observed, but rarely noted. William Shakespeare, a perhaps unmatched observer and cataloger of human behavior, once wrote about a "malady of attention." It is interesting to note, though, that he was speaking of an adult, not a child. But for the most part, behavior we'd now describe as symptoms of ADHD would historically be attributed to youthful exuberance or a simple lack of discipline or intellect.

The disorder didn't even have a widely accepted name until 1902. Pediatric orthopedist George Frederic Still had already made a considerable name for himself by then in the study of juvenile arthritis—Still's Disease, a degenerative bone disorder, is named in his honor. But while treating the bones and joints of thousands of children, he developed a consuming interest in their personalities and behavior. In a case study of 20 "problem" children at King's College Hospital in London, Still noticed his subjects to be to be "overly emotional," "lacking in inhibitory volition," and "lacking in the power of attention." He noticed they all engaged in exaggerated, "fidgety, almost choreiform [involuntary]" movement.

Still also found them to be "aggressive, defiant and [likely to be] cruel to others." Delving deeper, he observed that the children's behavior was not altered by punishment. Although he determined that the subjects had a "genuine fear of punishment," it did not prevent them from engaging in activities that they knew would elicit it. In fact, often times a child would go back to the activity he was punished for immediately after the punishment was over and in full view of the staff. One child in the study consistently stole items from the hospital and other children, then presented them to his parents, despite knowing that they would punish him.

Still was genuinely surprised by the consistently "mischievous, destructive, dishonest and spiteful" behavior the kids showed. And, as was customary at the time, he put the phenomenon in moralistic terms, referring to the disorder as a "defect of moral control."

Although he acknowledged that moral control—the ability to determine good from bad, and to act appropriately—was a taught skill and not something children were born with, he theorized that a defect of moral control was largely a physical problem. After he discounted any children from what he considered poor or ineffective parents from the study, all of the children in his study had some physical or inherited factor that he believed left them prone to behavioral problems. Many of them had a history of tumors, meningitis, epilepsy or significant head injury as infants or children. The remainder, he observed, came from families with a history of depression, alcoholism, suicide or, what was at the time a popular catchall diagnosis, "feeblemindedness."

Convinced that the root of undisciplined behavior was damage to the brain, he called his discovery "Post-Encephalitic Behavior Disorder." As a result, hyperactivity was associated with brain damage and, after the 1918 flu epidemic left millions of children with organic brain damage, the two became almost synonymous. As surely as a limp was the result of a leg injury or a congenital defect, so hyperactivity, a lack of discipline or even criminality—the thinking at the time went—must have come from head trauma or some inherited defect.

It was a fatalistic way of looking at things. Any child with behavior problems could blame it on a (perhaps forgotten) knock to the head or something inherited from a similarly luckless ancestor. The flipside of that concept was that any child unlucky enough to suffer a head injury or know of a questionable relative, could expect to lose at least some disciplinary control and would have to live with the accompanying stigma that came with the belief he or she would eventually lose control of their moral compass.

It wasn't until 1960, when a woman of towering intellect, immense courage and almost superhuman doggedness challenged that concept. Stella Chess was born to Russian immigrant parents in Manhattan's Lower East Side in 1914. She became a child psychologist in 1938, and later that same year, she married fellow child psychologist Alexander Thomas, who immediately became her collaborator.

After years of cutting-edge research, she became notorious, and then famous, after she challenged the all-powerful Freudian opinions of the time. She had a particular problem with the widely held beliefs that experiences such as weaning and toilet training were viewed as traumas that had profound effects on subsequent behavior. Injecting a little common sense to the argument, she wrote: "It seems incredible that a task accomplished routinely in most of the civilized and uncivilized world for a very long time could create so much worry in 20th-century Americans."

Her drive and reputation allowed her to undertake perhaps the most ambitious psychological experiment ever. Started in 1956 and continuing to this day, the New York Longitudinal Study of Child Development closely followed the lives of hundreds of children of various ethnic backgrounds and financial strata. Instead of studying a small group of children (Still had drawn his conclusions from a test of just 21 subjects.) with one characteristic and trying to figure out what caused it, she took a large cross-section of kids and studied everything about them.

She found that her subjects fell into three very broad categories: easy children, difficult children and slow-to-warm-up children. The difficult ones demonstrated the same symptoms that Still's "morally deficient" ones had. But while Chess acknowledged that such children could come from "adequate to excellent" parents as well as poor ones, she also found that many of them reported (or showed) no evidence of brain damage of any kind or any form of inherited fault.

Instead, she described these children as "hyperactive" because they carried out "activities at a higher rate of speed than the average child, or [were] constantly in motion, or both." Chess theorized that hyperactivity could be the result of any number of factors and that brain injury is just one of them. Although her ideas were quickly accepted in the United States, European doctors held on to the older idea that hyperkinesis (as they called hyperactivity) was always the result of injury or defect until the late 1980s.

Chess spent the rest of her life trying to help what she called "difficult" children. She wrote books with titles like *Know Your Child*, *Your Child Is a Person* and *How to Help Your Child Get the Most Out of School*. She continued the Longitudinal Study, maintained a private practice and worked as a professor at New York University's Child Study Center. When her husband and partner died in 2001, the university offered her emeritus status. She refused so that she could continue her daily work. Chess died March 14, 2007, aged 93. Her colleagues suspected as much because it was the first day in decades she didn't show up for work on time.

But while Chess and her colleagues did much to illuminate the dark world of hyperactivity, they couldn't figure out exactly what caused it. And, since nobody was sure what caused hyperactivity, there was little anybody could do about it.

At the time, the standard treatment was therapy. It wasn't all that effective, but there was little else they could do. Help came, ironically enough, from a stimulant.

Chemical stimulants were in high demand in World War II—every one of the major armies fed their soldiers amphetamine, methamphetamine or even cocaine to keep them alert and confident in the face of combat. Nobody denied that the drugs worked and, in the heat of battle, side effects were not considered important.

In 1944, a Swiss company called Ciba—later Ciba-Geigy, now part of the enormous Novartis firm—developed a new, easy-to-produce stimulant called methylphenidate (MPH).

Working on the same process as cocaine—preventing the brain's natural dopamine re-uptake hormones from doing their job, allowing the user to enjoy greater and longer amounts of dopamine, a hormone that increases energy and confidence—MPH was considered just one of the era's many wonder drugs. It lacked cocaine's immediate rush of euphoria, took longer to take effect, stayed in the body longer and was nowhere near as habit-forming.

After the war ended in 1945, many of these stockpiled stimulants were put to work in civilian markets, treating everything from narcolepsy and depression to impotence and the sniffles. MPH was put on the market under the name Ritalin in 1957.

Just like cocaine a few generations earlier, Ritalin was specifically prescribed to treat chronic fatigue, depression, psychosis associated with depression, and narcolepsy. Though effective for all of those purposes, Ritalin wasn't an immediate commercial success, largely because of the existence of cheaper and better-established amphetamine-based drugs serving the same purposes. Ritalin did find a niche in hospitals and rehab centers because of its ability to offset the sedating effects of other medications. It was especially effective and in demand for reviving the victims of barbiturate overdose—a significant concern as "downers" were a prominent recreational drug at the time.

But as Chess's theories about hyperactivity gained increasing acceptance, researchers looking for a treatment experimented with all kinds of drugs. Ironically, the only one that seemed to calm and slow hyperactive children was Ritalin, which they knew was a potent stimulant. Nobody knows for sure why Ritalin helps ADHD patients, but the prevailing theory now is that people with ADHD have more dopamine transporters than other people and that the excess of transporters starves the brain of dopamine by spreading it too thin. While the increase of dopamine may stimulate those without ADHD, it basically brings those with the disorder up to a place we might consider "normal."

Despite the side effects (which can include stunted growth and hallucinations) and the potential for addiction, Ritalin almost immediately became a popular prescription for children with ADHD. Doctors began prescribing Ritalin in the 1970s and usage steadily increased. As media attention portrayed Ritalin as the latest wonder drug, and as parents statistically spent less and less time with their children, usage exploded. From 1991 until 1999, sales of Ritalin rose by 500 percent, mostly in the United States.

While few deny that Ritalin works to control the symptoms of ADHD, a significant number of people (including many in the media and some medical professionals) have opposed what they feel is the rampant overprescription of the drug. And, since Ritalin acts as a powerful and admittedly enjoyable stimulant for those without ADHD, its prevalence has created an illicit market for the drug where none existed before.

I spoke with a psychiatrist I know from New York and asked him what he thought of Jason. He told me he wasn't stupid enough to try to pass a diagnosis on a child he'd never met; but that he would tell me a little bit about mental illness if I didn't use his name. He told me he had run into a lot of "problem children," especially when he was working in the emergency room of a busy urban hospital. "All children are a little self-centered, especially when they are stressed," he said. "But you can tell which ones don't care about anyone other than themselves."

He told me that kids who show many of the same symptoms Jason did may be lucky if all they have is ADHD, as it generally fades as the child gets older and they always have the Ritalin option. The same symptoms, the doctor told me, could be a reflection of something worse—something potentially much more dangerous and even less likely to respond to any form of treatment. And sadly, something statistically just as likely to occur as ADHD. The doctor from New York began to tell me about Antisocial Personality Disorder, or APD.

As the name obliquely implies, sufferers of APD have a problem with other people. While the existential philosopher Jean-Paul Sartre once famously wrote, echoing the frustrations of millions, that "hell is other people," people with APD don't occasionally get fed up with society; they just don't get it at all.

But it's more than that; specifically, APD is defined as a disregard for social rules, norms and cultural codes, along with impulsive behavior and an overall indifference to the rights and feelings of others. *The Diagnostic and Statistical Manual of Mental Disorders* (*DSMMD*), the bible of modern clinical psychiatry, indicates that a diagnosis of APD may be safely made if a patient shows just three of the following seven symptoms:

1. Failure to conform to social norms with respect to lawful behaviors as indicated by repeatedly performing acts that are grounds for arrest.
2. Deceitfulness, as indicated by repeated lying, use of aliases, or conning others for personal profit or pleasure.
3. Impulsivity or failure to plan ahead.
4. Irritability and aggressiveness, as indicated by repeated physical fights or assaults.
5. Reckless disregard for safety of self or others.
6. Consistent irresponsibility, as indicated by repeated failure to sustain steady work or honor financial obligations.
7. Lack of remorse, as indicated by being indifferent to or rationalizing having hurt, mistreated, or stolen from another.

Basically, a person with APD lacks empathy—the ability to care for or identify with others. He or she feels no guilt, no pangs of conscience after he or she has caused harm to others. Of course, if a person feels no guilt, it's much easier for them to commit crimes. And, not surprisingly, many serial killers and others who have profoundly offended society have been diagnosed with APD. But the *DSMMD* makes it perfectly clear that APD can not legally be diagnosed in patients younger than 18. Of course, this is to prevent confusing APD with ADHD, and to keep a child's life from being unfairly stigmatized by an incorrect diagnosis.

But that doesn't mean that children can't have APD, or show signs they'll develop it later in life. Back in 1963, a psychiatrist named John MacDonald published an article in the *American Journal of Psychiatry* called "The Threat to Kill." In it, he wrote about the data from his studies that showed that the overwhelming majority of murderers—and the frequency was higher among the more sadistic killers, the ones most likely to exhibit the traits of APD—shared three particular and peculiar traits. MacDonald found that the people who later exhibited severe criminal behavior and/or APD often wet their beds, set fires and exhibited significant cruelty to animals as children. While many children may experiment with animals—say, pull the wings off a fly to impress or repulse their peers—MacDonald made it clear that what he was talking about was real zoosadism, acts of cruelty to larger, more human-like animals such as cats and dogs, often alone and with the intent of pleasing the self and not others.

While any of these behaviors by themselves could be attributes to a lack of self-discipline or an excess of curiosity, when the three are seen together, they set off red flags among psychiatrists. They should; such notorious killers as Albert "The Boston Strangler" DeSalvo, John Wayne Gacy, Jeffrey Dahmer and others exhibited all of them.

But not everybody with APD exhibits the symptoms of the MacDonald triad, admits to them or is caught at them. The condition can be much stealthier than that. And those affected can be great liars. Often, a person with APD can blend into the rest of society seamlessly—or almost so. It can take the form of the overaggressive, nitpicking manager; the constantly interrupting and one-upping aunt; the co-worker who blames everyone else for his mistakes; or the housemate who raids the communal fridge at night. Since recent studies show that about 5.3 per cent of men and 1.8 per cent of women show the symptoms that indicate APD, it's not out of the question to surmise that we all know at least one, and most of us have one or even some in our family.

Traditionally, our culture has recognized two types of people with APD. The medical community, which nowadays shies away from calling people names, has largely abandoned these titles, but they are familiar to most people—sociopath and psychopath.

The difference is in presentation. A sociopath is someone who—often unashamedly—makes it clear that he or she has APD. We've all seen them. While lots of people will adopt outward signs of rebellion such as piercings, tattoos or a mode of dress, sociopaths usually make it pretty obvious they're not interested in your opinion of them, so much as they are interested in their own opinion of themselves. Our society has built up some collective and tacit knowledge of sociopaths—while there's no guarantee that a guy with a swastika tattooed between his eyebrows is dangerous, pretty well everyone is going to give him a little extra room on the subway.

But not all sociopaths are obvious by appearance. Some look very much like everyone else, but have clear behavioral cues. The doctor from New York acknowledges the difference between sociopaths and psychopaths, even if he doesn't use the names professionally any more. He tells me that if I want to see the difference between the two types, I should research the histories of two killers—Seung-Hui Cho and Ted Bundy.

* * *

If you hadn't known him, Cho would have appeared at first glance to be a fairly ordinary guy—a bit intense and aggressively nerdy, but within the bounds of what most people would call normal. But it became abundantly clear to Julian Poole, who encountered Cho in September 2005 when they were both juniors at Virginia Tech University, that Cho was anything but "normal." It was the first day of an American literature class and the prof was trying to break the ice and get to know his students by asking them to introduce themselves. Some were nervous, especially at first, and tried to get it over as quickly as possible. But most tried to get a laugh or sincerely offered some insight into their personality. When it came to be Cho's turn, he merely stared angrily at the prof. It was a horrible, awkward silence that seemed to last for a very, very long time. Finally, with a nervous chuckle and a long-forgotten disarming comment, the prof moved on to the next person. Later in the same class, the students were obliged to write their names on a seating assignment map. Poole, curious to learn the name of his silent and defiant student, noticed that Cho put a question mark where his name should have been. It apparently didn't escape the prof's notice, either. According to published reports, the school's faculty started referring to Cho as the "Question Mark Kid."

And he wasn't just that way in class. Karan Grewal, an accounting student who lived in the same undergrad suite as Cho in Harper Hall, knew him for months before he realized Cho could speak English. "It was weird that he never spoke, but we'd all got used to it," said Grewal, who only finally found out Cho spoke English when he peeked over his shoulder while he was furiously typing away on his laptop. "If you talked to him, he would stare down at his lap."

He generally didn't go to class either. Grewal couldn't recall much of Cho's behavior other than staring at the walls, typing away on his laptop and continuously riding his bicycle in circles in a nearby parking lot.

While Cho was strange as a junior, he was frightening as a senior. An aspiring writer, he took a poetry class taught by the distinguished poet Nikki Giovanni. While Giovanni is no stranger to tough situations, having been an important player in the civil rights movement and in early black activism, she was decidedly scared of Cho. She described him as having a "mean streak" and admitted that she was intimidated by him. She went to her department head, fellow poet Lucinda Roy, and complained about his habit of photographing female classmates' legs under their desks and of his "violent and obscene" poetry. Giovanni was so concerned that she threatened to resign her position if Cho was not removed from her class. Roy took these concerns to the school's chancellors, but they—ever mindful of litigation—told her there was nothing they could do unless Cho made a direct threat to someone, including himself.

A new Harper Hall roommate, Andy Koch, noted much of the same behavior from Cho that Grewal did. He saw the same repetitive, obsessive behavior—such as stabbing carpets and listening to Collective Soul's 1994 hit "Shine" continually for hours on end. The unusual conduct became even more apparent once Koch realized that Cho had taken something of a shine to him. One morning, he woke up to find Cho taking photographs of him. Later, he received a barrage of rambling, incoherent cell phone calls from Cho, who claimed to be an imaginary brother named "Question Mark." This was the same name Cho used when talking to girls he was attracted to, though he invariably creeped them out enough to make them want to have nothing to do with him.

Women were a big problem for Cho. Koch described a number of run-ins Cho had with uniformed Virginia Tech security guards, each of them the result of a woman's complaint that Cho was stalking her. When Cho finally did talk one day, the first thing he told Koch was that he had a girlfriend. At first, Koch was relieved, until Cho told him that his girlfriend was a supermodel named Jelly and that she lived in outer space. He wasn't joking; he wasn't being sarcastic; Cho really did expect Koch to believe in his extra-terrestrial paramour.

Things got worse when Cho intercepted an instant message address of one of Koch's female friends. He sent her a few incoherent messages and then he nailed a piece of paper with a quote from William Shakespeare's *Romeo and Juliet* to her door. It said: "By a name, I know not how to tell who I am. My name, dear saint, is hateful to myself, because it is an enemy to thee. Had I it written, I would tear the word."

The young woman thought nothing of it until she received a message from Koch, warning her about Cho. He told her all about his prior stalking arrests and wrote to her: "I think he is sch[iz]ophrenic, or however you spell it." Alarmed, the young woman called campus security. Familiar with Cho, the campus cops dropped by and gave him a verbal warning. Cho then texted Koch, threatening to commit suicide.

Unsure of what to do, Koch called his dad. Astutely, his dad told him to call campus security, which he did. Just to be sure, Koch's dad called them too. The security officers apprehended Cho, served him with a temporary detention order and escorted him to the New River Valley Community Services Board, a mental health facility in nearby Blacksburg.

Cho did everything to convince the doctors there that he was mentally healthy and not suicidal, but they determined he was "an imminent danger to himself and others" and referred him to detention at the larger, more intensely secure Carilion St. Albans Behavioral Health Center farther along the road in Christiansburg. The psychologist who treated him there, Dr. Roy Crouse, considered him "depressed," but noted that he denied thoughts of suicide and decided that "His insight and judgment are normal." He recommended Cho be treated on an outpatient basis. On the strength of Crouse's findings, Special Justice Paul M. Barrett signed a judgment that Cho be freed on the condition that he accepted follow-up treatment. He visited the facility just once after that, and no progress on his condition was reported.

Cho got up for school early on the morning of April 16, 2007. He had big plans that day and, to accomplish them, he brought along two handguns and hundreds and hundreds of hollow-point rounds of ammunition—the type of bullet that does by far the most damage to human tissue. While a normal bullet will pass through anything it hits largely intact, hollow points collapse on impact, creating large, flat surfaces that bulldoze their way through the human body. The difference in damage is enormous.

A few hours and hundreds of shots later, Cho had killed 32 Virginia Tech students and faculty and wounded another 25, before killing himself.

Courtesy Joanne Champagnie

Johnathon Madden's sixth-grade school portrait, taken shortly before he died. At 12 years old, Johnathon was about five feet tall and weighed about 100 pounds.

Courtesy Tonia Cowan

Kevin and Johnathon Madden lived with their mother, stepfather and another family member at 90 Dawes in Toronto's east end. The boys shared a bedroom behind the window on the upper left.

Courtesy Tonia Cowan

The backyard of 90 Dawes. The window on the right is where Kevin confronted his stepfather, Ralston Champagnie, before letting him in the house.

Courtesy Damian Langton

Ashley and Pierre both attended Rosedale Heights School for the Arts.

Courtesy Hewitt Langton

After the murder, Kevin and Pierre hid and then spent the night in nearby Taylor Creek ravine. They emerged from the other end of the park the following morning.

Courtesy Tonia Cowan

Both Kevin and his friend Pierre were arrested at the corner of Coxwell Avenue and O'Connor Drive, not far from the murder scene. Identified by a concerned commuter, the boys were arrested by separate sets of police officers at about the same time.

Lucas Oleniuk/*Toronto Star*

The jeans that Ralston struggled out of were still in front of 90 Dawes the day after the murder. The police left them and other evidence in place until forensics experts finished their investigation of the crime scene.

Lucas Oleniuk/*Toronto Star*

The presence of police and emergency vehicles at 90 Dawes drew attention from people in the neighborhood, especially school-age children—many of whom were familiar with Johnathon, Kevin or both.

Courtesy Toronto Police

Kevin's mugshot. After a year in custody, he appeared in court much trimmer, but his behavior was still very immature.

Tim's mugshot. He was arrested at home while Kevin and Pierre were still hiding out.

Courtesy Damian Langton

Tim Ferriman was held at the Syl Apps Youth Centre in Oakville, Ontario, not far from Toronto. Kevin, however, was held at Sprucedale Youth Centre, a more secure facility about 90 miles away in Simcoe, Ontario.

Courtesy Toronto Police

Investigators found three potential murder weapons at 90 Dawes. Though much of the testimony involved the green-handled butcher knife (bottom), at least one expert claimed that the meat cleaver—with its distinctive notch—must have been involved.

© *National Post*

Reporter Joseph Brean discovered Ashley's blogs and wrote about them in a front-page article for the *National Post*. His revelations forced a second trial.

Alex Urosevic/*Toronto Sun*

Robert Nuttall defended Kevin in both trials. He argued that the brutality of the attack indicated that Kevin was not in control of his actions at the time.

Dave Thomas/*Toronto Sun*

Dennis Lenzin represented Pierre in both trials. He described his client as "shy" and "non-confrontational," claims that were backed up by witnesses and Pierre's behavior in custody and in court.

Dave Thomas/*Toronto Sun*

Detective Sergeant Terry Wark was the lead investigator in what the media called the "Jonathan" case. After the second trial, Wark spoke on behalf of Joanne and Ralston.

Tannis Toohey/*Toronto Star*

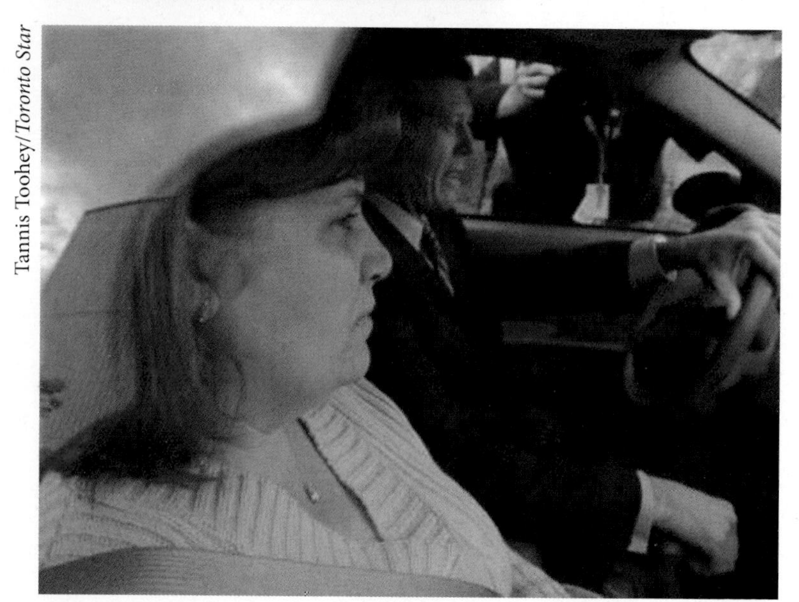

After the verdict came down in the second trial, Wark drove Joanne home. It was 27 months after the murder and not long before what would have been Johnathon's 15th birthday.

While Cho's case is complex and interesting for a number of reasons, there are two aspects of his story that make his a very good example of sociopathic behavior. The first is that he didn't think he had done anything wrong. In fact, it appears that he considered himself something of a hero.

During a break in his shooting spree, Cho sent a package via FedEx to NBC. It contained a number of photographs and videos of him posing with his guns and knives and trying to look cool; but, more important, it included a manifesto of sorts. In it, he wrote: "All the shit you've given me, right back at you with hollow points." He railed against what he considered the sinful habits of his classmates and compared himself to Jesus Christ. He absolved himself of all responsibility, writing:

> When the time came, I did it. I had to. You had a hundred billion chances and ways to have avoided today, but you decided to spill my blood. You forced me into a corner and gave me only one option. The decision was yours. Now you have blood on your hands that will never wash off.

Later, investigators found a note in his dorm room that denounced the other students at Virginia Tech as "rich kids" and "deceitful charlatans" whom he felt he had to punish for their "debauchery." In a sentence that appears to sum up his motive, he wrote: "You caused me to do this."

While the world was horrified by the day's events, there were those at Virginia Tech who weren't surprised at the killer's identity. "I knew when it happened that that's probably who it was; I would have been shocked if it wasn't," Giovanni told reporters after the massacre.

"That's the thing about Cho," the doctor from New York said, when I spoke to him later. "Everybody knew he was different, he was strange, he was even potentially dangerous; but what could they do about it?"

It's true, after the murders, nobody—not even Cho's family—really tried to deny his sociopathy, nobody pretended he was just a misunderstood guy. It was universally acknowledged that he was a very sick young man and that his sickness was abundantly obvious, but there was little anybody could do to help him. He wouldn't seek help because he was convinced there was nothing wrong with him; it was, in his opinion, everybody else who was at fault. Because of privacy laws and other civil liberties concerns, there was little the university could do but encourage him to seek help. The nature of his problem meant that he was unlikely to trust, tell the truth to, or confide in the medical professionals trying to help him—which, of course, defeats the purpose of therapy. His family, though, repeatedly tried to intervene. Deeply religious people, they prayed for him and brought him to church regularly, but to no avail. "Mental problems aren't like other physical problems," the doctor told me. "You can't just clean the wound and apply pressure like you would a hemorrhage; it's much more complicated than that—and, unlike a hemorrhage, you can almost always deny it."

* * *

As much as Cho is a definitive example of a sociopath, Ted Bundy was a classic psychopath. Invariably described as handsome, charming, articulate and educated, Bundy used his superficial charm to seduce or at least temporarily gain the trust of women. Once they were alone with them, he would bludgeon, strangle and rape them, often after they died. While he eventually confessed to 30 murders, some—particularly those in law enforcement—are convinced there are more.

Bundy, originally from Vermont, had a childhood love of skiing that led to a habit of shoplifting items he couldn't afford. He started by stealing small items, then moved up to skis and other equipment, eventually developing the nerve to forge ski passes and even lift tickets. He was arrested twice as a minor, but those records have been destroyed and he appears to have done no time in jail.

He was popular as a youth, despite being a compulsive liar and admitting, "I didn't know what made people want to be friends. I didn't know what underlay social interactions." This sort of revelation is not uncommon among psychopaths. Without the ability to care about other people, psychopaths are unable to understand or express many common emotions like grief. This was well illustrated when Nicole Kidman was preparing for a role as a psychopath in the film *Malice*. She turned to Dr. Robert Hare, a professor emeritus at the University of British Columbia in Vancouver and one of the world's leading authorities on psychopaths. Hare, who has written extensively on the subject and has consulted with the FBI, RCMP and other agencies on criminal investigations, told her to imagine a scenario:

> You're walking down a street and there's an accident. A car has hit a child in the crosswalk. A crowd of people gather round. You walk up, the child's lying on the ground and there's blood running all over the place. You get a little blood on your shoes and you look down and say, "Oh shit." You look over at the child, kind of interested, but you're not repelled or horrified. You're just interested. Then you look at the mother, and you're really fascinated by the mother, who's emoting, crying out, doing all these different things. After a few minutes you turn away and go back to your house. You go into the bathroom and practice mimicking the facial expressions of the mother. That's the psychopath: somebody who doesn't understand what's going on emotionally, but understands that something important has happened.

As a student at the University of Washington, Bundy learned a lot about human behavior, not just through his studies in psychology, his major, but also by volunteering on the night shift of Seattle's suicide prevention hotline. It's as though he made a conscious effort to study how non-psychopaths behave.

While at school, he had his first-ever relationship with a woman and was crushed when she dumped him for being "too immature." Many of the academic, law enforcement and media professionals who have studied Bundy since agree that this crisis impacted him so hard emotionally that it changed his psyche permanently. Not long after, he entered into another relationship.

He also became more successful financially. After graduation, he began to work for the Washington state Republican Party and became closely associated with Governor Daniel Jack Evans. More confident, he approached his original girlfriend and began dating her again, along with the new one. When he proposed to the first girlfriend and she happily accepted, he broke the relationship off, refusing to give a reason or even accept her phone calls. Later, he told psychologists: "I just wanted to prove to myself that I could have her." He continued dating the second woman, who later said she also would have accepted an offer of marriage, at least until Bundy ran into legal trouble.

In the summer of 1975, police in Colorado saw Bundy's VW Beetle driving around in a quiet suburban neighborhood in the middle of the night with its headlights turned off. Thinking it was an ordinary traffic violation, the police attempted to stop him by flashing their lights. He floored it. Shocked that anyone in a VW would try to outrun a police car, with a V8 engine the officers gave chase. When they caught him, they searched the car and found handcuffs, a crowbar, an ice pick, pantyhose with eyeholes cut out of them and other items police and courts often associate with crime. They also noted that the front passenger seat was missing.

About a year earlier, November 18, 1974, an 18-year-old woman named Carol DaRonch was working in a mall in Utah when a stranger, a handsome man, walked in and told her someone was trying to break into her car. She followed him out to the parking lot and later recalled she assumed he was a mall security guard because "he was so in control of the situation." Although the car seemed okay, the man (who identified himself as "Officer Roseland") asked her to accompany him to police headquarters. Suspicious, she asked to see some ID. He quickly flashed a gold-colored badge and she got into the backseat of his VW Beetle. She found it odd that the front passenger seat was missing, but didn't say anything.

He drove in a direction she knew was opposite the police station. He eventually stopped in a vacant parking lot and tried to put handcuffs on her, accidentally locking both cuffs on one wrist. DaRonch screamed. The man pulled a handgun, pointed it at her head and threatened to shoot her if she screamed again.

She didn't remember later how she did it, but DaRonch managed to open the car door and fall to the ground. The next thing she knew, he had picked her up and slammed her against the car. He held her with his left hand and had a crowbar in the other. He was threatening to bash her head in when she kicked him in the testicles. The man went down in a heap and she ran, eventually flagging down a car driven by an elderly couple. They took her—crying hysterically and with the handcuffs still hanging from her wrist—to police.

Bundy was soon arrested for DaRonch's kidnapping on the basis of her description of him and his car. Despite the fact that he had been positively identified by her in a lineup, was shown to have the same type of blood she had on her coat, and that he had no alibi, Bundy was confident he would win the case.

He was wrong. Bundy was found guilty and sentenced to one to 15 years in prison, with eligibility for parole.

Almost as soon as he landed in prison, Bundy underwent a psychiatric evaluation. With some astonishment, the doctors found that Bundy was not "psychotic, neurotic, the victim of organic brain disease, alcoholic, addicted to drugs, suffering from a character disorder or amnesia, and was not a sexual deviate." They did, however, decide that he had a "strong dependency on women" and, perhaps more important, a "fear of being humiliated in his relationships with women."

The strange *modus operandi* of the DaRonch kidnapping attracted the attention of law enforcement nationwide and Bundy was soon suspected of murder. On December 22, 1976, he was charged with the murder of Caryn Campbell, a woman who had disappeared in January of 1975 while vacationing in Colorado with her fiancé and his two children.

Bundy had made a great issue in the media about how poor he considered his lawyers to be, and said that he was thinking about representing himself in the Campbell case. He eventually managed to gain permission to visit a law library in nearby Aspen. For these trips, he asked for and was granted permission to wear civilian clothes so as not to draw attention to himself. On one of these visits, while the guard wasn't looking, Bundy leapt from a second-story window and ran to freedom.

Aware that the police would set up roadblocks around the city, he stayed in Aspen, stealing food and sleeping in empty holiday cabins. On one of his foraging trips, he ran into an armed man who was part of the search party looking specifically for him. He managed to talk his way out of the situation and the man let him go. He was free for six days before two sheriff's deputies spotted him in a stolen car weaving in and out of traffic. From then on, he was obliged to wear handcuffs and leg irons on his trips to the library.

Wary, the state placed him in a smaller, more secure jail. Using nothing but his abundant charm, he managed to convince a fellow inmate to give him a hacksaw blade and $500 in cash. He escaped again. He stole an MG, but the tiny roadster stalled in the deep mountain snow. Stranded, he hitched a ride to Vail and took a bus to Denver, then a flight to Chicago. He then took a train to Ann Arbor, Michigan. He went to a bar that night and watched his favorite team—the Washington Huskies—beat the hometown Michigan Wolverines 27-20. He spoke to a number of people that night, some of whom even bought him drinks, and—despite the nationwide manhunt—nobody identified him. He then stole a car, drove to Atlanta and took a bus to Tallahassee, Florida. It was a place he later said he loved because of the intellect and youth associated with the city's Florida State University. He even sat in on a few lectures. While there, Bundy also committed a number of minor crimes and attacked six women, murdering three, including a 12-year-old who he raped and disposed of in a pigsty.

Bundy later approached a 14-year-old girl who was waiting for her brother to pick her up from school. Bundy told her he was from the town's fire department and wanted to talk with her. He picked the wrong girl. This one happened to be the daughter of the Jacksonville Police Department's chief of detectives and he had warned her about such people. She was suspicious of an on-duty firefighter in plaid pants and a navy blazer, so she ignored him and did her best to keep a safe distance. When her brother eventually showed up, she told him the story and they memorized the license plate number on the white van Bundy was driving.

The police visited the man the plates were registered to, and he showed proof that they had been stolen. Suspecting the worst, the children's father showed them a book of mug shots. Both of them, in separate rooms, identified Ted Bundy as the man with the van.

Bundy ditched the van and stole an orange VW Beetle. Sensing the area was becoming aware of him, he drove west. As he passed through the then-sleepy town of West Pensacola, a police officer noticed the unfamiliar car and ran the plates. They came back stolen.

Again his slow VW was overtaken and, as the officer tried to handcuff Bundy, he fought his way free and ran. The officer shot at Bundy, who lay down, pretending to be hit. When the officer arrived to check him out, Bundy attacked him again, only to be overpowered and arrested again.

Defending himself, Bundy put on a great show in court. At one point he proposed marriage to one of the defense witnesses, his former co-worker Carole Ann Boone, and she accepted. Since both were under oath at the time, it counted as a legally binding contract. Despite fighting for his life against a staggering number of rape and murder charges, Ted Bundy managed to get married on national TV.

But he was ultimately convicted, largely because his teeth perfectly matched the bite marks on many of the victims. After the guilty verdict was returned, Bundy claimed that media misrepresentation was responsible for the decision—it was all their fault.

On one of their many conjugal visits, Bundy and Boone conceived a daughter, Tina. A series of appeals went nowhere and an offer to help find the notorious Green River Killer did nothing to alter his sentence. When Bundy was eventually put to death by electric chair on January 24, 1989, his final words were: "I'd like you to give my love to my family and friends."

"That last line really kills me," the doctor from New York told me. "Even though he was dying—had nothing more to gain or lose—he was still playing the game, pretending to care about his family and friends, when it was abundantly obvious that he didn't."

Indeed, the doctor believes (and this seems to be a consensus about Bundy) that Bundy was absolutely incapable of caring about anyone other than himself. His dying words were emblematic of his desire to be perceived as someone who did care, though.

* * *

Bundy is a crystallization of what differentiates a psychopath from a sociopath—his or her ability to mimic the outward signs of being a caring person. Early in his life, Ted Bundy realized that if he wanted to get what he wanted—eventually the total control he enjoyed through torture, murder and sex with corpses—it would be easier to get if he pretended he was "normal." By looking like a regular, even desirable, guy he could gain the trust of and, therefore, access to women that an obvious sociopath like Cho could only dream about. While Cho repulsed the women around him with his desperate overtures, calm cool Bundy had his pick of them. In fact, all of his victims had the same look—long, dark hair parted in the middle with no bangs, because that was his favorite hairstyle.

"If you really want to get down to brass tacks, a psychopath is a smarter—or at least more pragmatic—sociopath," the doctor from New York told me. "While the sociopath makes his illness obvious and scares off the people he most wants to be in contact with, the psychopath lures them in with a veil of normalcy, even exceptionality."

That's the problem with psychopaths; they blend in among us. Most of them, according to the medical literature I've read, come across as confident, charming, friendly and intelligent. Not only is it hard to identify them, it's hard not to fall under their spell. And if you think that their victims come from the weakest, most needy or least intelligent sectors of our population, you may want to think again.

"Psychiatrists are often helplessly manipulated by the psychopath," says Dr. Ken Magid, a clinical psychologist and author of *High Risk: Children Without a Conscience.* "Just as are the psychopath's other victims." While a sociopath won't seek help because he or she denies the problem, the psychopath not only denies the problem, but has learned the ability to hide it from others, including the doctors who could potentially help them.

Of course, the doctor from New York reminds me, not all psychopaths are serial killers. It just doesn't make mathematical sense. While people with APD make up maybe four percent of the population, murderers are a tiny fraction of that and serial murderers are a tiny fraction of them. What, I ask, do the other psychopaths do?

"Well, I know one of them who works at a Lexus dealership," says the doctor.

He's only half-kidding, but he makes a point. Dr. Robert Hare calls psychopaths who don't break laws (or at least don't get caught and punished) "subcriminal psychopaths." Psychopaths in our society can be the dashing cad, the Type-A personality, the two-timing boyfriend or just an otherwise ordinary person who puts themselves before others. Dr. Sheila Wilson, a psychiatrist who works with the victims of psychopaths, points out that psychopaths often prey upon the weaker members of our society, and neither side may realize it. A psychopath who pays excessive attention to an emotionally needy person, for example, will find it much easier to borrow money from them and is unlikely to pay it back. But it's not just the needy who can be targets. "Psychopaths play on the fact that most of us are trusting and forgiving people," says Michael Seto, a psychologist at Toronto's Centre for Addiction and Mental Health.

There's nothing close to a consensus as to what causes a person to become a psychopath. At a time when the prevailing wisdom was that people who demonstrated this type of behavior were invariably the product of a poor, abusive upbringing, Hare postulated that what made psychopaths act the way they did was physical. He couldn't point to exactly what made their wiring different, but he was sure it was.

"Nobody believed him thirty years ago, but Bob hasn't wavered, and now everyone's where he is," says Dr. Steven Stein, a psychologist and

CEO of Multi-Health Systems in Toronto. "Everyone's come full circle, except a small group who believe it's bad upbringing, family poverty, those kinds of factors, even though scientific evidence has shown that's not the case. There are wealthy psychopaths who've done horrendous things, and they were brought up in wonderful families."

And, since nobody knows what causes a psychopath to be a psychopath, treatment options are limited. According to Seto (a doctor at a facility dedicated largely to rehabilitation), by the time a psychopath hits his or her late teens, the condition "is almost certainly permanent."

Over the years, various treatments have been tried out on psychopaths with sadly consistent results. No drug seems to make a difference and therapy rarely does. Therapy requires the patient to recognize they have a problem and psychopaths rarely do; it also requires honesty and psychopaths, having practiced deception their whole lives, are unlikely to change their behavior in such a situation. Besides, "psychopaths don't discriminate who it is they lie to or cheat," says Seto. "There's no distinction between friend, family and sucker." So what's a doctor but another sucker to be used? The psychopath will talk with the therapist, say all the things he or she feels the doctor will want to hear, and often comes out of the sessions with a passing grade, although no progress has actually been made.

In fact, the treatment may actually do more harm than good. "Psychopaths often con the system, including the therapists and, ironically, may be more likely to re-offend after receiving current prison treatment programs," said Hare. In one of his studies, psychopaths who underwent social-skills and anger-management training before release had an 82 percent reconviction rate, while psychopaths released from the same institution who didn't take the program had a 59 percent reconviction rate.

Frustrated by the lack of effectiveness of their treatments, the Correctional Service of Canada (CSC) in 1991 asked Hare to design a treatment program. He worked on something totally original. Instead of, as had historically been the case, appealing to the psychopath's guilt or remorse (which they don't even have) by trying to make them feel bad about what they'd done, Hare suggested that treatment be based on appealing to the psychopath's all-important sense of self-interest—as in, look what your actions have done, they've gotten you in jail, so it must have been the wrong plan. It made perfect sense. Instead of wasting time, energy, money and opportunity trying to get a person unable to feel guilt to suddenly do so, Hare wanted to teach psychopaths to follow our rules because it was in their best interest. But by the time he finished the proposal the following year, there was a new team in charge of the CSC—and they didn't like Hare's plan at all.

He recalls that they told him his proposal was unfeasible because, as they pompously told him, "we don't believe in the badness of people." That's it, book shut, program dead.

"The irony is that Canada could have had this all set up and they could have been leaders in the world," he said, now that many of his ideas are being adopted worldwide. "But they dropped the ball completely."

CHAPTER 5

# big brother, "vampire boy" and friend go to court

A little more than a year in custody didn't seem to have hurt the boys at all. A supervised diet and mandatory exercise helped Kevin lose some of his excess poundage, slimming him from obese to merely overweight. The same regimen had the opposite effect on Pierre, who was no longer painfully skinny and had filled out considerably. Tim had grown his hair long and arrived in court with a ponytail.

The victim, all three accused and many of the witnesses were all under 18, which prevented the media from naming any of the people involved. Instead, they began to refer to trial as the "Jonathan" case, using the more conventional spelling of the victim's first name. In news reports at the time, Kevin was usually called "the victim's brother," while Tim and Pierre were called his "friends." Once the facts of the trial began to emerge, though, the media unfailingly referred to Tim as "Vampire Boy."

It was December 2, 2005, and the trial had been going on for about two weeks. Up until that day, there were hearings to determine if plea bargains could be made (they couldn't), jury selection, what kind of trial the boys would have and where it would be held. Since most of what had happened up to that point had been procedural, the boys had become bored by their long court appearances, often listening to lawyers talk for hours about things they didn't understand or didn't really care about. While occasional items would appear to pique their interest, Kevin and Tim spent much of their time daydreaming, doodling and joking around with each other. Pierre, on the other hand, consistently remained quiet and focused. His mother and father showed up every day, and the entire family appeared to be following each word of the case as intently as any of the lawyers and the judge.

But that afternoon, Tim was paying extra attention. Ashley—looking pretty and likeable in a blazer and skirt suit—was on the witness stand. A year away from her had given him a different perspective on the girl he once proclaimed his undying love for. As she spoke, he sneered at her and wrote her name surrounded by the word "bitch" on the yellow legal pad he was supplied with. He hated her for ratting on him, for taping their phone call and for sending his e-mail to the cops.

Crown Attorney Hank Goody is a small, energetic man who is always perfectly coiffed. He has an extra sense for details and a flair for the dramatic—he seems tailor-made to lead the prosecution in a high-profile murder case. He had already warmed the jury up by reminding them that Johnathon had been "stabbed, cut and chopped 71 times."

He told them about the tape and how it had been made by a team of frightened and concerned girls, including Ashley. Goody addressed the jury directly and told them: "By their own words which you will hear spoken in their own voices, you will know that the three young persons before you now were responsible for Johnathan's death."

Then he pushed play on the tape recorder. The recording begins with the electronic purr of a phone ringing from the caller's side. There's some murmuring. Then Kevin answers. Goody played the entire tape Ashley had made without stopping. The courtroom fell silent. The jury was aghast. Even Kevin stopped goofing around and paid attention.

To some it seemed like nothing less than the kind of courtroom confession you see in movies or on TV. All three boys say quite plainly that they intend to kill that day, and two of them identify the planned victims, with Kevin specifically mentioning the murdered boy. Pierre only obliquely talks about his part in the plan, laconically answering "since today," after Ashley asks him "Since when do you kill people?"

The tape appeared to say that the boys had promised her five murders and delivered on one.

Goody wisely waited for the effects of the tape to sink in on the jury before questioning Ashley again. He established that she had made the tape after she had received a similarly distressing call earlier in the day. He asked her why she taped the second call, which seemed to him an odd thing for someone her age to do. She replied: "To make sure this wasn't a total lie or joke."

On the following day, Goody then questioned Heather, at whose house the tape was made. She told the court about how the girls had hatched the plan in drama class and repeated Ashley's belief that they needed hard evidence of what the boys were planning before they would be taken seriously. "We didn't want to worry anyone unless we had evidence," she said. "We didn't want to blow this out of proportion in case it was a practical joke." She seemed a bit embarrassed when Goody asked her if she had ever taped phone calls before and admitted she had, but just for fun.

Then Goody brought Heather's mom to the stand. She testified that the girls seemed extremely agitated when they arrived at her house and ran upstairs that day. Heather gave her instructions that they were not to be disturbed because something "very serious" was going on and that she couldn't tell her what it was until they had it all figured out. "Frankly," the mother told court, "I thought one of them was pregnant."

When the call ended, the court heard, the girls "freaked out." Heather dashed down the stairs, explained the situation to her mother and played her the tape. Her mom immediately called 911.

Police officers Paul Wildeboer and Glenn Gray corroborated all of the day's testimony.

* * *

The next day, two of Johnathon's friends were called to the stand. Dressed in a black Nike hoodie and jeans, 11-year-old Jeffrey was questioned by the judge, David Watt, as to his understanding of the legal system and the importance of his testimony. He passed the judge's approval.

Jeffrey described Johnathon's life in glowing terms. He spoke about how the two of them played and talked and shared interests, about how they did "almost everything together." Then Jeffrey detailed the last time he saw Johnathon. It was the afterschool snowball fight on the day Johnathon was murdered. After a short detention when school was finished, he told the court, Jeffrey ran outside. There he saw Johnathon with Jamal (a younger boy he would later escort home) and another boy about their age. Goody asked him if he went straight home, as he lived just across the street from the school. "No," the boy said excitedly. "We had a snowball fight." His enthusiasm drew a laugh from the audience when he described Johnathon as being hard to hit because he was "moving around like something out of *The Matrix*."

Jeffrey then testified that his mother called him in to punish him for coming home when he wasn't supposed to earlier in the day. Jeffrey had a short debate with his mother in which he asked if he could go to Johnathon's house. She said no. Jeffrey complained a little but accepted his fate. Johnathon told him he was going to take Jamal home and go to the cyber café.

Later, Sean, Johnathon's older friend, painted a similarly idyllic picture of the boy's life. He talked about how they played basketball and other sports together and how they had been friends for as long as either could remember. Sean told a story about how Johnathon's mother had taken them to the annual Santa Claus Parade about a week before he died.

He then recounted the events of November 25, 2003 as he saw them. Johnathon's class got out late, so Sean played basketball with other friends. Later, he still couldn't find Johnathon, so he went home. Sean called his best friend's house, but he got Kevin, whose voice he recognized, who told him Johnathon wasn't home. Bored, Sean went to the cyber café himself, hoping his friend would show up. Eventually, he did. But Johnathon was out of money and Sean had just spent the last of his, he testified.

"What did he do then?" Goody asked him.

"He left," Sean replied.

"Did he come back?"

"No."

"Did you ever see him again?"

Sean paused and then said: "No."

Goody asked him what he did after Johnathon left. Sean told the court that he played the rest of his game and at a time he estimated to be 5:20, he left for home. He pointed out that he could see Johnathon's house from the corner as he passed Dawes on the way home.

"Did you see anything there that night?" Goody asked him.

"Yeah," Sean replied. "There were lots of police cars."

* * *

The next witness to speak was the neighbor whose house Ralston ran to after the attack. He testified that Ralston was pantless, bleeding profusely from the head and screaming that Kevin (who the man knew) had "tried to stab him with a knife and his friend hit him on the head with a baseball bat."

The witness then told the court that he was a friend of Ralston's and saw the Champagnie family frequently. He noted that in the summer he would often invite the whole family—except for Kevin—over for barbecues. When asked why he didn't invite Kevin, the witness said that he didn't like Kevin and Kevin didn't like him.

Indicating that he had a plan, Goody asked the witness what color his skin was. The witness was black. Ralston is black. Kevin, Joanne and almost everybody else involved with the case are white. Johnathon was also white.

But if Goody hoped to convince the jury that part of Kevin's problems with Ralston were because of racism, the judge was having none of it. He told Goody to stop asking questions based on race, saying that he had "no idea" how it was relevant to the case.

The police officer who responded to the neighbor's call, Constable Stephan Charron, testified that he took Ralston's report, which included the initial attack by Kevin and the subsequent assault by Pierre. He also noted that Ralston had told him about the condition of the house and the presence of, and hasty exit by, Tim.

* * *

On the following day, the court heard testimony from the ETF officers who arrived at 90 Dawes and then eventually at Tim's apartment. Constable James Hung, the team's leader, described how he and his team "cleared" the house, using a battering ram to enter the building, shouting warnings before making any moves and using a mirror on a stick to see if anyone was in a room before entering. He told how the officers cleared the first floor room by room, moved first upstairs and then down to the basement. Hung described how he and his officers were unable to avoid stepping in the vast pool of blood at the bottom of the basement stairs and then had to trudge through the broken beer bottles. Goody then asked Hung if he knew what he'd find down there. "On going down, there was a bit of urgency," he said. "We didn't know what was in the basement—we couldn't avoid it."

Constable David Leck, an eight-year veteran of the ETF, was the first one down to the basement. He described following the blood trail over the broken glass to the crawlspace. It was slightly open, and Leck could see that there was a person inside. "It was a body; I alerted the team," he testified. "I called out to the body. There was no response."

Paramedic Ron Bogle testified that the police directed him to the crawlspace and he saw a child's body in full fetal position. "I could see blood all over the body," he said. Immediately, Bogle checked for vital signs: "I couldn't find anything." Aware that he could not help the child in the crawlspace or the basement, he wrapped him up in what paramedics call a "drag sheet"—a specially designed blanket with handles intended for the safe and quick transport of severely wounded patients.

Goody then questioned Atilla Bodo, Bogle's partner, who had already treated Ralston before seeing Johnathon. Bodo saw the body and immediately thought the worst. "He was quite evidently vital signs absent." The 16-year veteran paramedic noted that one of Johnathon's eyes had a "fixed, dilated pupil" (not a good sign), while the other eye was swollen shut due to a large gash just above the eyebrow. It was just one of many "large, irregularly shaped lacerations" Bodo noticed on the boy. Although most were on the head and neck, there were also a few defensive wounds on the hands—one finger on his right hand was nearly severed. Those wounds, he testified, did not compare to those on Johnathon's neck. Bodo told the court that the boy's trachea was completely severed. He placed a cardiac monitor on Johnathon; it detected no signs of life. Normally, at that point, paramedics give up on trying to revive patients, but because Johnathon was so young, Bodo testified, he made what he called a "last-ditch effort." He inserted a laryngoscope—a device that allows a medical professional to look down the throat of a patient—into Johnathon's mouth, but he couldn't see anything he could recognize. He was shocked to see the light from the scope shining on the opposite wall of the ambulance. Eventually, Bodo desperately inserted the laryngoscope directly into Johnathon's open throat wound, but it was no use.

Bodo testified that he asked Bogle to call Sunnybrook Hospital at 7:03 to ask for assistance. At 7:07, he said, he had no choice but to declare Johnathon dead.

Earlier, Hung testified that they had just finished "clearing" the house when they received a call that one of the suspects had fled to another address—Tim's apartment.

One of the other ETF officers who testified that day was Constable William Cook, who actually arrested Tim. He told the court that the team had assembled in Tim's back yard with shields and shotguns and were ready to break into the house when they were surprised. The back door opened, he said, and the officers could see Tim, with a mobile phone in his hand, just inside the apartment. Cook testified that he repeatedly ordered the boy to put the phone down and put his hands on his head, but Tim ignored him. Instead, the cop said, Tim walked toward the team "with a blank look on his face."

His actions, Cook said, "forced" the police officer to kick the boy in the ribs to immobilize him. "I wasn't sure of his mind-set at the time," he said. Then he paused and added: "I believe it knocked a little wind out of him." Some of the audience, comparing the hulking cop to the skinny kid, chuckled a little.

Cook also noted that another man—who appeared to him to be in his late 20s—emerged from the apartment and started arguing with and then threatening the officers. He too, was placed under arrest. Tim, according to Hung, identified the older man as his father and told him in front of the police that he had witnessed a murder.

Tim's defense lawyer, David McCaskill, had little of substance to ask Hung, Cook, Bogle, Bodo or any of the other officers who were at 90 Dawes on November 25. It's generally considered bad form at a jury trial for a lawyer to contradict or get at all rough with people whose jobs it is to save lives, especially when they have already delivered heart-wrenching testimony. Still, McCaskill did ask Cook if a kick to the ribs was the most appropriate way "to take down a 15-year-old boy." Unruffled, Cook replied that "under the circumstances," it was.

* * *

Next came the testimony of the officers who arrested Kevin and Pierre. Detective Constable Chris Sherk described his surprise at seeing the suspects "just strolling down the street." Even as he and his partner approached, Sherk said, Pierre looked "very relaxed—he didn't seem worried." Sherk then said he "took physical control" of Pierre and, once he confirmed his identity, placed him under arrest for first-degree murder. He waited for a reaction from the boy, but none came. "It struck me as very strange, like it was no big deal," the detective testified. "I guess if somebody told me I was under arrest for murder, I might exhibit some emotion."

Detective Sergeant John Rossano told a very similar story when it came to his arrest of Kevin. When the murder suspect appeared to be "devoid of any reaction," Rossano decided to make sure Kevin was aware of what was happening to him. "Do you understand what this is about?" Rossano said that he asked Kevin. "Yeah," he testified Kevin answered. "The death of my brother."

The next witness to take the stand was Detective Constable Robert Armstrong, from the Toronto Police forensic identification unit. He processed Kevin and Pierre after their arrests. His testimony included photos of the boys from the night of the arrest. Although Kevin was much fatter and had a more aggressive hairstyle in the photo, it was clearly the same boy. Armstrong then showed photos of Kevin's right hand, which revealed fresh bruising and lacerations on the knuckles and on the heel of the palm. Armstrong testified that Kevin's wounds were from "fairly recent" activity. He showed photos of both boys' knees and one of Pierre's back. His back was covered with a series of deep, reddish welts perpendicular to his spine. At least one courtroom observer I spoke with later admitted that it appeared as though Pierre had been whipped, but Armstrong testified that they were just stretch marks, the result of Pierre growing so quickly that the skin on his back just couldn't keep up.

Armstrong also catalogued what the boys had on them when they were brought to the police station. Pierre had on a black baseball cap, a black Perry Ellis jacket, a white "Deep in Denial" T-shirt, blue Mecca jeans, plaid boxer shorts and a pair of white K-Swiss sneakers. Kevin wore a similar uniform with a black faux leather jacket, a red "Just Do It" T-shirt, striped boxer shorts, black fleece sweatpants and black and silver Adidas sneakers. Neither boy carried any cash, but Pierre had a monthly student bus pass in his black nylon wallet and a house key.

Armstrong noted that both T-shirts were stained with a dark substance, which, he testified, "I took to be blood."

As was the case with the other police officers, Armstrong testified that he was surprised by the boys' lack of reaction to their situation. He described them as "compliant and cooperative" and said, "they seemed unconcerned" about their predicament.

* * *

Armstrong's colleague from the forensic identification unit, Rick McKeown, took the stand the next day. The leader of the crime scene investigators at 90 Dawes, McKeown showed the court a number of photos of the scene and evidence found there. He began his testimony with a description of the deep pool of clotted blood he found at the bottom of the stairs and the spatters of blood on the adjacent walls. "It all appeared to be low to the ground," he said.

Next to the pool, he spotted two stacks of white plastic chairs. On top of one of them was what he described as "a large hunting knife" with a black handle.

Throughout the basement, he noted broken glass, mostly green but some clear, some with labels identifying them as pieces of beer bottles still attached. On the glass, he noted a great deal more blood. "My opinion was the glass was broken before the blood got deposited on it," he testified. McKeown also noted mustard splatter marks throughout the basement and a TV that had recently been smashed in.

Upstairs in the house, in the front hallway near the main entrance, McKeown testified that there were two baseball bats—one wood, one aluminum—resting against a wall. "There appeared to be blood spatters on both," he said, noting that the aluminum one was much bloodier. He also pointed out that there was mustard on both of the bats. Beside them, on the carpet, was another blood spatter.

A thorough search of the house revealed a large, notched meat cleaver partially sticking out from under the living room couch, a green butcher knife in the kitchen beside a series of more blood spatters and a bloody towel in the blood-stained main floor bathroom sink.

He revealed that there were no identifiable fingerprints of any of the suspects on the bats, knives or meat cleaver.

On the following day, McKeown showed the court a photograph of the faded jeans Johnathon was wearing the day he was killed. On them he pointed out a number of mustard stains that matched the mustard spatters in the basement. He then moved on and pointed just above the left knee and said, "On the center portion of the left leg, we see brownish red discoloration, which appears to be dried blood."

That was too much for Joanne, who had been very composed up to this point. The sight of her dead son's tiny jeans—ones she had handled countless times before—stained with his own blood and the mustard from the boys' rampage hit her hard. Maybe she was picturing him being dragged over the broken glass or maybe it just reminded her that her boy was gone, but it caused her to break down. She was taken from the courtroom in tears.

She didn't have to see the next exhibit, which was Ralston's shredded winter jacket. It may well have saved his life when it absorbed the force of the butcher knife Kevin had thrust at his heart.

* * *

After a break for the holidays, court resumed on January 4, 2006. The first witness called was Robert Gerard of the Center of Forensic Sciences. The Center, operated by Ontario's Ministry of Community Safety and Correctional Services, is a central facility for forensics and is used for both criminal and civil cases. He testified that the mustard found on the floor, the bats, and Johnathon's pants matched the stains found on Kevin's pants and Pierre's pants and left shoe. He also said it was the same mustard found on Tim's shoes, T-shirt and pants.

* * *

With most of the physical forensics out of the way, the prosecution started to paint pictures of the personalities of the people involved. The first was a girl—we'll call her Katie—who claimed to have been Kevin's girlfriend. She was nice-looking enough, but not as well turned out as Ashley and her friends. She wore tight jeans, a turtleneck and hoop earrings, which she could not stop fiddling with.

Goody asked her if she was nervous. Katie giggled and said she was. He asked her how long she had known Kevin. "We started going out in Grade 8," she told him.

He asked her if she considered herself Kevin's girlfriend at the time. She replied that she did. The girl then described their relationship by saying "we hung out a lot." She testified that she had been to 90 Dawes on many occasions and that she knew Ralston, Joanne and Johnathon well. While she was there, Kevin usually played video games—he had a remarkable collection not just of games, but of systems, she said—but she didn't play very often because he was so much better at them than she was.

Goody asked her if she knew Tim and Pierre. She said that she had met them both on separate occasions. He asked her if they seemed to get along well with Kevin. She said they did.

Goody then asked if Kevin seemed close to his family. She said he didn't. "He didn't talk to them much about his personal life," she answered. When he spoke to her about his family, it was always to complain.

Goody asked why she felt a need to break it off with Kevin. She told him that Kevin had sent her and some other students threatening notes—hers said "Die, bitch"—after the two of them had an argument about her involvement with another boy. A teacher phoned the police and the girl was interviewed about the matter. She didn't know of any aftermath.

When Goody was finished with her, Kevin's lawyer, Robert Nuttall, asked her: "Do you recall that Kevin had expressed some suicidal thoughts about killing himself?"

"I didn't know about that," she answered.

"Were you aware that he had been hospitalized at a psychiatric hospital for about a week?" he asked.

She shook her head and said she wasn't.

The next witness was Ralston, who was questioned about his relationship with the boys. He said that he and another family member had moved in with Joanne and the boys in January 1997. Johnathon was not quite six and Kevin was 10. Ralston and Joanne were married that summer.

He told the court how his relationship with Johnathon was fine, but that Kevin had become increasingly problematic. He described for the court how the older boy refused to do his share of the household chores and would not accept any criticism. Kevin rarely spoke, and when he did it was usually just to complain. Ralston then related an anecdote that fairly summed up the closeness he had developed with Johnathon and the gulf that had emerged between him and Kevin.

About a month before the murder, Ralston had visited a doctor to have a benign cyst removed from the back of his neck. He was at home recuperating when Johnathon arrived. The boy noticed that his stepfather was bleeding from the site of the operation and asked if he was okay. Ralston explained about the procedure and assured the boy he was fine and just wanted to relax. Johnathon promptly got him a towel for his neck and then made him dinner. When Kevin arrived home, he wordlessly ate what remained of Johnathon's cooking, then went up to his room. Ralston told him to do the dishes, Kevin refused.

Things had gotten so bad between them that they barely spoke to one another. Ralston described how he had even attended counseling and eventually handed over his share of Kevin's discipline and punishment to Joanne. "I just couldn't take it anymore," he said.

But it was that night when Kevin wouldn't do the dishes after Johnathon had been so kind that enraged Ralston enough to break the deal he had made to leave discipline to Joanne, and punish Kevin. He banned the boy from using the family computer. "I told him he was grounded from the computer," he testified. "Because he loved the computer the most."

Goody asked him if there was anything else odd about Kevin at the time. Ralston told the court that Kevin had complained about being beaten up at school, although he showed no evidence of any assaults and was much bigger than any of his classmates. Still, Ralston took him seriously and suggested that they contact the police. He testified that Kevin told him that if they got the police involved that Kevin would be murdered. Ralston let the subject drop.

Then Ralston was asked to describe the day of the killing. He testified that Kevin was very angry at him. The original ban from the family computer had been extended because Ralston had caught Kevin using it when he wasn't supposed to be.

He then described how Kevin had kept him waiting outside the back door, despite the cold, and how they'd had a small argument about the smoke and wine glasses in the house.

After a night's recess, Ralston took the stand again. He described in harrowing detail the attack Kevin and Pierre visited upon him after Tim fled. In a loud voice and with animated actions, he told how Kevin first stabbed at him, then wrestled him to the ground. He talked about how Pierre had swatted him in the head with a baseball bat several times. He described how he kept struggling for his family's sake. "I almost gave up," he told the court he recalled thinking at the time, "Jesus Christ! This is the way I'm going to die?"

Ralston then told the court about his escape, how he slipped out of his jeans and flagged down a bicyclist before heading to a friendly neighbor's house for safety. He also testified that he found out about Johnathon's death later that night while recuperating in a hospital bed.

Although Ralston's story was exciting, plausible and fit in with what the police and other witnesses had to say, he struck many in the courtroom the wrong way. Three different observers have since told me that there was something about him that seemed less than credible. "He seemed so adamant, so angry [and] like he had practiced his story too many times," one told me. "And he seemed to get mixed up easily on facts and figures, particularly time."

Perhaps surmising that Ralston's testimony could be the prosecution's weakest link, Kevin's lawyer, Robert Nuttall, cross-examined him intensely. Quickly, he revealed that Ralston had a long history of drug- and assault-related arrests and had sought treatment for narcotics abuse. Nuttall then tried to paint the interior of 90 Dawes as a threatening place of anxiety and stress with Ralston, not Kevin, as the primary reason why. He asked Ralston if Joanne had been hospitalized for slitting her wrists after an argument with him. Ralston admitted that she had.

He also admitted that he would occasionally use his slippers to discipline Kevin when he was younger, but he drew the line at Kevin's claim that Ralston had hit him with a plastic baseball bat, leaving a nasty bruise.

Then Nuttall asked Ralston if he had ever punched Kevin in the head at a birthday party, as the boy had claimed. Ralston denied it. Kevin said that he had told a teacher about the incident, which prompted a visit from the Children's Aid Society.

"Do you remember back when Kevin was 10 years old that the Children's Aid Society came to have a little chat with you about a suggestion that Kevin had made to a teacher that you had struck him?" Nuttall asked.

"I don't remember that part," Ralston said. He also denied Kevin's claim that he beat him up for reporting the incident to his teacher. But he did agree that Kevin's problems and his own problems with Kevin were the reason they attended family counseling. He admitted that in one of these sessions, Kevin told him: "Once or twice when I disciplined him it felt like abuse, and I said to him, 'If that's what you feel, I'm very sorry.'"

"Do you recall Kevin being angry at his mother for her failure to protect him from you?" Nuttall asked.

Ralston said he didn't.

Nuttall pressed on: "Did you also call him names, names like 'stupid fuckhead'?"

Ralston denied that and also Nuttall's assertion that he and Joanne neglected Kevin while showing unlimited and unconditional love and affection for his little brother.

Finally, Nuttall asked Ralston if Kevin had any reason to try to stab him that day. Ralston said he didn't.

Ralston also faced Dennis Lenzin, Pierre's lawyer, that afternoon. Lenzin suggested that Pierre hit Ralston with the bat because he was trying to break up a fight between them. Ralston had, after all, admitted to scuffling with Kevin. Perhaps Pierre was just trying to save his friend Kevin, who had said he was calling out "help me" during the fracas. Ralston denied it.

Lenzin then wondered aloud how a man who had been attacked with an aluminum baseball bat had gotten off so lightly. He then suggested that the boy had hit him four or five times. Ralston said that he was hit at least that many times in his head alone.

Lenzin sneered and asked him why then did he only have "a bump on the head and a sore thumb?"

Ralston seemed flustered and then weakly added: "There was also a scratch on the chest."

* * *

If Lenzin had tried to minimize and potentially discredit the injuries reported by Ralston, he wouldn't dare with the next witness. Dr. Michael Pollanen is Ontario's chief forensic pathologist and a well-respected member of the scientific community. He has been asked to work on cases as wide-ranging as a UN inquest looking for evidence of systemic government-sponsored torture in East Timor, and the alleged murder of Ireland's soccer coach, Bob Woolmer, in Jamaica. No scientist is infallible, but Pollanen's expert opinion is as authoritative as any in the country.

He told the court he'd received Johnathon's body at about 11 o'clock on the morning of November 26, 2003. It was wrapped in a sheet inside an official body bag.

He described Johnathon's body as being that of a normal, well-nourished prepubescent Caucasian boy. He was about 4-feet, 10-inches tall and the doctor estimated him to be a shade less than 100 pounds in life. He had short sandy brown hair, brown eyes and a few freckles. He was still dressed in a T-shirt, football jersey, sweatshirt, boxer shorts, blue jeans and black socks. He was not wearing shoes.

Pollanen's initial examination discovered 71 "sharp-force injuries"—a catch-all term covering any type of assault with a bladed weapon, including stabbing, hacking and slashing. The body showed a number of bruises, some from the everyday life of a 12-year-old boy, others from the attack. The face was so badly traumatized that the doctor said he had a hard time making out his facial features.

As he described the 71 wounds, Joanne first began to sob and then had to be taken from the courtroom. The three accused, however, betrayed no emotion other than boredom.

Pollanen went on. He said that 55 of the wounds were to the head. He described them all as "perimortem"—so close to the time of death it's hard to determine if they were inflicted just before or just after. Some of them were surface wounds. One, beneath the left eye, scraped the flesh off the cheek, exposing the bone. Many of them, he said, had scratched Johnathon's skull and some of them had actually pierced the bone, going all the way into his brain.

Goody asked him if he could tell how much force was required to make such a wound. Rather than describe it in terms of pounds per square inch or other statistics, Pollanen deadpanned: "Sufficient force to perforate the skull."

But as bad as they were, Pollanen said that the 55 head wounds were almost certainly not what killed the little boy. Instead, it was the three profound wounds to his throat that proved lethal. One of them sliced through the muscles of his neck to completely severe his larynx, rendering him unable to make a noise. The thrust was powerful enough to make an indentation on the bones in the back of his neck. With his windpipe severed, Johnathon could no longer breathe through his mouth or nose. He could get air through the open wound, but with it came a great deal of blood.

Johnathon's lungs were rapidly filling up with blood, but that's not what Pollanen testified killed him. The doctor said he could immediately tell from the color of Johnathon's body that he died from catastrophic blood loss. He testified: "At the time of death he had a very small amount of circulating blood in his body."

He also noted eight "sharp-force" wounds on Johnathon's fingers. He noted that they were what are often called "defensive wounds," indicating that he probably instinctively tried to use his hands to defend himself from the onslaught. Pollanen also noted "perimortem" bruises on Johnathon's arms, back and chest, which would be consistent with him being restrained during the attack. There were also abrasions and lacerations on his thighs, which were inflicted postmortem. Pollanen said they could have been the result of his body being dragged over broken glass.

In the cross-examination, Tim's lawyer, McCaskill, presented Pollanen with a hypothetical re-creation of events. He surmised that Johnathon received superficial injuries after someone knocked him down the basement stairs. Then the right side of his head could have been held against a wall while he was attacked with a bladed weapon in "a rapid and continuous fashion," explaining why 42 of the 55 head wounds were on the left side of his head.

Pollanen agreed that the scenario was plausible.

Then McCaskill asked him if one of the three potential bladed weapons found in the house—in particular the green-handled knife, as opposed to the black-handled knife and the meat cleaver—could have been used to inflict all 71 wounds.

Pollanen said that it very well could have, but his opinion was that the murder weapon was more likely the black-handled knife, which the police found on the stack of plastic chairs near the bottom of the basement steps.

Then McCaskill asked Pollanen his opinion of the blood spatters at the bottom of the stairs. The expert witness testified that when Johnathon's voice box was slashed, the blade also severed the carotid artery—the major blood vessel that brings blood from the heart to the brain—and that the markings on the wall and floor were consistent with such an injury.

Lenzin, Pierre's lawyer, asked what Johnathon would have experienced after his throat was cut in such a manner. Pollanen said that his body would have gone into shock. Lenzin asked him to explain what that meant. Pollanen testified that a person in that type of shock "can expect to feel cold, dazed, confused and ultimately unconscious."

* * *

The next important witness was a bit of a surprise. Goody's partner Anna Tenhouse called Christopher Dicks, a guard at a youth court in Scarborough where some preliminary hearings for the boys were being conducted. He had overheard a conversation between the boys that he and Tenhouse thought was significant.

By that point of the trial, the boys had shown very distinct but consistent attitudes. Kevin showed little interest in the trial, often daydreaming or staring off into space. Tim would often doodle on his notepad, glare at Ashley and her friends, and generally goof off while the trial was on, and then joke around with Kevin during recesses. Pierre, on the other hand, paid very close attention to the proceedings, became emotional at some of the more grisly moments and demonstrated many different signs of nervousness, from shaking his leg to biting his nails. He tended not to join in Kevin and Tim's jokes and conversations.

Dicks testified that at the preliminary hearing in Scarborough on April 8, 2005 Pierre showed symptoms of a panic attack. "He couldn't stop biting his nails," he said. "His hands were holding his head; his knees were shaking." It got so bad the judge was compelled to call a recess.

Dicks testified that as he and another guard were escorting the boys from the courtroom, he heard Kevin say: "What's wrong with you? I have never seen you have two panic attacks in two days before." He described Kevin's tone as one of "disbelief."

Dicks then told the court that he heard Pierre snap back at Kevin: "Yes you have. I was there when it happened and I don't want to relive it again."

* * *

Goody called another expert witness from the Ontario Centre for Forensic Sciences, DNA scientist Cecilia Hageman. She had tested blood samples from Johnathon's body as well as the stains on Kevin's red T-shirt and black sweatpants and Pierre's jeans. She testified that the chances that the blood on the clothes came from anyone other than Johnathon were about "one in 820 billion."

She also testified that Johnathon's DNA was found in blood stains on the green-handled knife, both baseball bats and on the basement wall near the basement stairs, the stack of chairs beside them, on the first-floor washroom sink and on the stove in the kitchen.

Hageman also said blood stains matching Ralston's DNA were also found on both Kevin and Pierre's clothes.

She was followed by Robert Wood, chief of forensic dentistry for the Ontario Coroner's Office, who testified that he reconstructed a model of Johnathon's head to give him a better idea of where his wounds were and how they were most likely inflicted. His findings indicated that the meat cleaver was at least one of the weapons used in the attack on Johnathon. Many—at least 30—of the wounds about his head and neck showed consistencies with the cleaver, which had a distinctive notch in the blade.

* * *

Then came the star witness, again. Ashley looked very pretty in her business-like blazer and skirt ensemble. Although she maintained an air of decorum and gravity, she managed to dazzle the entire courtroom with her one shy smile. Ashley was so instantly likable that one observer at the trial later told me that Tim did himself no favor by glaring at her and repeatedly writing "bitch" on his legal pad big enough for both the judge and jury to see.

Goody began his questioning by asking her about the first phone call she received from Kevin's house on the day of Johnathon's death. He wanted to know what was so frightening about it that it made her call back and tape the second call.

Ashley said she was "disturbed" by the call. Goody pressed her as to why, he asked her to take him and the court through the call. Ashley testified that she was home in bed because she had called in sick that day. She had been trying to end her three-week romance with Tim, but he just couldn't seem to accept it. When he called, he was crude and a little bit abusive: he was clearly showing off. Ashley said that she heard the voices of two other boys. Goody then asked her what Tim said that offended her. Tim asked Ashley if her mom (whom he'd never met) was "hot," if her older brother had ever been raped and if she knew that "people shit their pants when they died."

After that last recollection, Joanne started crying.

Ashley continued her testimony. She said that she heard the beep of call waiting, excused herself from Tim and answered the other call. It was her dad, calling to check up on her because she had taken the day off school, telling her parents she was sick. She assured him she was okay, then went back to Tim. As she reconnected, Ashley overheard him tell someone else that he was "not going to be home tonight or ever."

She asked him what he was talking about. Tim told her that she could find out what was up by watching the news "that night or tomorrow morning."

When she asked him what he meant by that, she testified that he screamed: "It doesn't concern you, bitch!"

She told the court that his abuse made her want to hang up, but she didn't because she heard Tim ask his friends if he could tell her about what they had planned. Goody pressed her on. "And they responded, 'As long as she doesn't tell,'" she told him.

Intrigued, Ashley stayed on the line. Tim unveiled his plan. At that point, Tim spoke of a plot to kill Kevin's family. Further, he told Ashley of a long-range plan. She testified: "He told me they were going to steal all the parents' credit cards and buy bombs and ammunition and suicide bomb either malls or highways."

Goody asked her why she didn't go to her parents or the police. Ashley told him that she didn't think the police or her parents would take her very seriously. Goody asked why not. She replied: "I didn't have any evidence."

* * *

Cross-examining so jury-friendly a witness as Ashley could be hazardous for the defense lawyers. If they appeared to be too rough on her, it could easily turn the jury against them. But up until this point, the case had appeared open and shut. The overwhelming weight of evidence supported the theory that the boys, led by Kevin, brutally murdered Johnathon and attempted to kill Ralston. Hell, the jury had already heard them—all three of them—on tape telling Ashley that they were planning to do as much.

The defense team's only hope, it would seem, would be to discredit Ashley's testimony. To make it appear as though Tim, at least, and also perhaps Pierre, were trying to impress her with fabricated stories of murder and mayhem, not knowing that some of it would actually happen. Kevin was clearly a lost cause—let him try an insanity defense—but Tim and Pierre had a chance to be portrayed as puffed-up young men eager to impress a pretty young girl with tales of what they took to be manliness. It wouldn't take much to convince the jury that Tim and Pierre were stupid and deluded; the real challenge would be to get them to believe that Ashley could be impressed—even turned on—by their nihilistic claims. If they could prove that Tim and Pierre were only pretending to be murderers because they thought it would make her like them better, they had a chance of painting the two younger boys as blameless—if not entirely innocent—stooges.

McCaskill, Tim's lawyer, dove in and asked her if she believed Tim's claims that he was a vampire. "I didn't take seriously that he was killing people in the Don Valley," she answered.

He asked if it was true that Tim had drunk her blood. Ashley sighed. She told the court that she and Tim were messing around at her house—her parents weren't home—and they were throwing some fruit, she recalled they were pomegranates, at each other. One of his throws went wild and she tried to catch it with a plate. The plate shattered, and one of the pieces made a small slice in her forearm. Before she knew it, Tim was at her arm, licking up the blood. She told the court that she found it disgusting. Blood was his thing, not hers. As if to put an exclamation point on the statement that buried Nuttall's argument, Ashley told the court that Tim's interest in blood and violence was what made her want to dump him in the first place. That stuff was just too weird for her.

McCaskill then asked what the entire courtroom was wondering—what did a beautiful girl with all the advantages in life ever see in a loser like Tim? "He was nice to me most of the time," she answered. Ashley then said that she only liked Tim for "about four or five days."

"And after that?" McCaskill asked.

"I didn't like him anymore and I had wanted to get out of the relationship," she answered. "My friends didn't like him—I didn't like him."

Again he brought up the fact that Tim told her that he drank blood. Ashley deftly told him that she didn't take that seriously, that she didn't take much of what Tim said or did seriously. That he was the kind of boy who spoke in the voices of his favorite cartoon characters. McCaskill asked what that was about. "Fourteen-year-old boys tend to talk like that," she said with a sigh. Some members of the jury laughed.

He asked her to describe their relationship. "He thought he was in love with me," she said. McCaskill asked her if she was in love with him. She looked at him as if he was crazy and then said she wasn't. In fact, she said, she "found him silly" and "told him pretty much blatantly that I didn't want to see him anymore."

McCaskill then asked her why she didn't end the relationship earlier then. She told him that she couldn't. When she tried, she testified, Tim got angry and started breaking things. She tried to let him know subtly, to give him hints that she wasn't interested in him, but he was, she maintained, "too dense" to pick them up.

She hadn't seen him for about a week before Johnathon died. But he'd called her the day before. She told the court that she was just stringing him along when she told him she'd see him the next day. When he got in touch with her via MSN Messenger that day—the day she called in sick—she made up a story about how there were workmen at her house and he couldn't come over.

They then skipped to the second call from Kevin's. McCaskill asked her why, if she was so disturbed, did she go to see her school friend instead of her parents. Ashley told the court that Heather "takes me more seriously than my mother does."

At McCaskill's urging, Ashley then detailed how the girls went to Heather's house, called Kevin's house and taped the boys. The jury had already heard the tape and knew what she was talking about. McCaskill asked her if she did anything to try to stop the boys from putting their plan into action. Ashley admitted that she no longer wanted Tim to be her boyfriend, but she still cared about him as a person. She told the court that she offered to meet Tim somewhere away from Kevin's. The tape backed her up. She then said that Tim refused, telling her: "I have to kill somebody today." Again, her account was corroborated by the tape.

After that, she testified, it was out of her hands. Heather took the tape downstairs and played it for her mother, who called the police. While this was happening, Ashley testified, she was still upstairs, crying.

McCaskill asked what happened after that. Ashley testified that Tim called her back. McCaskill asked her what he said. She told the court that Tim had told her: "I wanted to let you know that if anything happens to me—if I go to jail or anything—I want you to know that I love you."

If the boys' lawyers wanted to unnerve, upset or discredit Ashley, they did a terrible job. She left the stand as she arrived, pretty, popular and utterly believable.

* * *

The next witness, Dr. Dominique Bourget of the Royal Ottawa Hospital, testified about Kevin's mental state. She examined him after the arrest in a series of interviews in Ottawa. She said that he was of "about average" intelligence and suffered from no brain abnormalities or injuries. But there were many aspects of his personality that lead her to decide that he was "quite disturbed."

He told her that he had almost no contact with his biological father, who had abandoned the family on Christmas Eve when Kevin was just eight years old. She also testified that he said his stepfather, Ralston, physically and emotionally abused him frequently. He also spoke of a mounting resentment for his mother as a result of her inability or lack of desire to protect him from Ralston's abuse.

Kevin told her that he had very little success at school, in sports or at any other activity other than perhaps video games. Despite this, Bourget testified that Kevin had a feeling of grandiosity—excess self-importance. She said he demonstrated "hostility, attitudes of bitterness, social alienation and distrust of others" in their interviews and as she described it, his life was "going nowhere." He had been encouraged to seek professional help for his psychological state many times, but, Bourget testified, "he has a history of minimizing reporting of his own mental condition."

That alienation sent him into what she called a "marginal subculture," along with other troubled youths. With them, she said, Kevin experimented with Satanism and vampirism. He admitted to her that he and Tim had tasted each other's blood.

Bourget testified that Kevin had told her that he had woken up "pissed" on the morning of November 25, 2003 and that "he felt angry for no particular reason" and "basically felt like breaking things."

Alone in the house, he slept in late, took a shower and headed downstairs. Before long, Pierre showed up. Kevin had told Bourget that the two had skipped school together frequently and that Kevin was not at all surprised to see him. The pair then went upstairs to the room Kevin shared with Johnathon and played video games.

While they were up there, she continued, Tim called and told them he had been stood up by his girlfriend. Kevin invited him over and he showed up a few minutes later. After he arrived, the boys started to drink red wine and smoke cigarettes. Bourget testified that Tim egged on Kevin's bad mood and encouraged him to let his frustrations out. Bored with the video game and emboldened by Tim, Kevin then took the boys downstairs, smashed the mustard jar, beer bottles and TV. With the three of them riled up, Kevin told them to ransack his parents' room, to look for money, identification and credit cards. They took what little money they found to a nearby convenience store, bought snacks and cigarettes and returned to 90 Dawes.

That's when, Kevin told Bourget, Tim suggested he call Ashley. He was pissed off at her and, emboldened, wanted to give her a piece of his mind. At first, Kevin was against the idea, but relented because Tim had told him about her interest in vampirism and Kevin thought that she might be impressed by their boldness that day.

About three hours later, Johnathon came home to get his money to take back to the cyber café. Kevin told Bourget that something Johnathon said—Kevin couldn't recall it exactly—indicated that Johnathon was going to tell Ralston about the mess Kevin and his friends had made. That "set him off." Johnathon's words, Bourget testified, "triggered a rage state" in Kevin. He told her that he "grabbed a knife, ran to his brother, pushed him down the stairs and ended up attacking him." He told her that he was alone in the basement with Johnathon during the stabbing. He described the attack as "a dream-like state" and told her that he could only recall stabbing his little brother once, despite the 71 wounds he suffered.

"What happened between 1 and 71?" Goody asked.

She replied that Kevin was undergoing an "emotional surge" and totally lost control of what he was doing. She said that people in that state "can't stop the impulse." She also pointed out that while Kevin did not remember all the events of killing his little brother, he did admit he had done it.

Bourget then testified that she asked Kevin about the link between the phone call in which all three of the boys boasted they would kill Kevin's family and the fact that he later killed Johnathon. He described it, she said, as the "worst and biggest coincidence of his life." He claimed, she said, that the call was just typical teenage boasting and he hadn't planned to kill anybody.

Not long after the attack on Johnathon, Ralston came home. Kevin told Bourget that after Tim left the house apologizing and Ralston found evidence of Kevin's smoking and drinking, his stepfather attacked him. Ralston was, Kevin told her, choking him when Pierre tried to fight the older man off with a baseball bat. After Ralston gave up his attack and ran out the front door, the two boys fled and spent the night in a nearby ravine.

Under cross-examination, Bourget was asked to typify Kevin's mental state, to put a name to any psychological disorder he might have.

She said that Kevin told her about episodes of depression, anger and violence, during which he enjoyed an adrenalin rush. He also told her that "anything in his way, objects or people, was a target." When asked what triggered these bouts, the doctor replied: "The episodes happened when he felt everything was falling apart for him—a loss of control in his life."

Bourget was asked if Kevin's problem had a name. She said it was called "Intermittent Explosive Disorder." But she warned that it was a temporary diagnosis. When Nuttall asked what that meant, she replied that Kevin could have any number of mental disorders developing, but it was too early in his life to diagnose them accurately. She gave her testimony four days before Kevin's 18th birthday.

* * *

The first of the accused to take the stand was Tim. He looked pale, thin and nervous. He began his testimony by describing his life before the attack.

He hadn't seen his mother since he was two years old. He told the court that she'd dropped him off at his father's apartment one day and never come back to get him. He was doing very poorly in school because he cut classes so frequently. He freely admitted to being a petty thief and habitual vandal. And, when asked, he admitted that he had a "fetish" for drinking blood and that he had told more than a few other kids that he'd killed people in the Don Valley to drink their blood. Asked if he'd describe himself as a vampire, he replied that he would.

Tim then detailed his brief romance with Ashley. Though he admitted that it was "going downhill" by the day of the attack, he thought it was still salvageable. He was delighted that she had agreed to see him that day, so excited in fact that he called her at 8 o'clock in the morning. She told him it was too early and that he should call back later. In order to be marked on the official attendance list as present,

Tim then went to school for his first class, then left. He immediately went to a nearby cyber café (not the same one Johnathon went to) and played some video games. Asked to describe them, Tim said they were "shooting games" with "terrorists and stuff." Tiring of them, he logged on to MSN Messenger and saw that Ashley was online. He asked if it was okay to come over now. She replied that he couldn't come over that day at all.

Angered, he testified that he pulled out his cell phone and called an old friend he hadn't talked to for a long time. It was Kevin. He too was cutting class and had another friend at his house with him. Kevin then invited him over.

When he arrived, he let himself in and went up to Kevin's room. Among other small talk, he testified that he asked Kevin why he hadn't seen him for more than a week. Kevin told him he was "depressed" and explained that it was because his family was bothering him. Although Kevin often complained about his family, Tim testified, he was "more intense" than usual on that day and revealed for the first time that his stepfather had physically abused him. Tim told Kevin that Ashley had blown him off earlier that day. "Sucks to be you," his friend replied.

Goody asked Tim about the rampage in which he, Kevin and Pierre smashed the bottles and TV. Why he had gone along with it. Tim seemed bewildered at the question. "I always broke things," he eventually replied, "so it just came natural to me."

He testified that when Johnathon came home and saw the mess they had made, he told Kevin that he was going to tell their parents because he didn't want to be blamed.

Tim then said that Kevin then dragged his little brother down the stairs to the main floor and let him go at the top of the basement stairs. As Johnathon turned around to walk down the stairs, Kevin knocked him to the bottom, ran down the stairs and begun stabbing his little brother.

His lawyer, McCaskill, asked him what he was doing during the attack. "I didn't say or do anything," he said, trembling visibly. He then described how he could see Johnathon trying in vain to protect himself with his hands as Kevin just kept slashing. "I could barely believe what I was seeing," Tim testified. "I was shaking very violently and felt very nervous."

McCaskill asked him where Pierre was. Tim told him he was in the living room, not watching.

Then, he said, Kevin—still fuming and red-faced with anger, his hands covered in blood—came up the stairs and told him to help hide the body. Tim added that the knife in Kevin's hands was pointed at him, but did not say that Kevin was actively threatening him. McCaskill asked him if he helped Kevin, if he dragged Johnathon's body over the broken glass and then stuffed him the crawlspace. Tim admitted that he had. He said he complied because "I'd just seen Kevin kill his little brother and I didn't think he'd think twice about killing me."

McCaskill then asked Tim if he'd taken part in the killing, encouraged Kevin to kill Johnathon or even if he knew Kevin was planning to do such a thing. He said no to each of the questions.

Goody got tough with him. He told him that he believed that Johnathon was just the first of the family they planned to kill that day. "You planned to get Johnathon out of the way before Ralston came home," he said.

Tim denied it.

"You were worried about the timetable," Goody said.

"We weren't worried about any timetable because there wasn't going to be a murder," Tim said.

After helping Kevin move Johnathon, Tim testified that all he could think about was getting out of the house. His chance came, he said, when Kevin's stepfather came home. Tim apologized repeatedly to Ralston and slipped out the front door as the man turned to confront Kevin.

After he left the house, Tim said, he ran away, eventually catching a bus for home. After a couple of stops, Kevin and Pierre got on the same bus and sat near, but not with, him. They acknowledged one another, Tim testified, but did not talk. Kevin and Pierre got off the bus after a brief ride and Tim said he saw them go into Taylor Creek Ravine.

When he got home, Tim said, he did not tell his father what had happened because he didn't want him to "freak out." Tim said he was going out the back door of their apartment to make a phone call when he saw a dozen shotguns aimed at him. He claimed he didn't realize they were police officers until they arrested him.

When he was asked about the phone calls he made to Ashley in which he boasted that he, Pierre and Kevin were going to kill Kevin's family, he too claimed it was just a coincidence. "I made it up," he told the court and added that the boys did not discuss killing anyone before the call. "I was trying to impress her." When asked what happened after she rebuffed his advances to come over, Tim told the court: "I kind of felt like an idiot."

* * *

Although she cried frequently in court and sometimes had to be led out of the room during testimony, Joanne maintained her composure admirably when it was her turn to speak, despite allegations that she showed so much preference for Johnathon that Kevin felt neglected and ignored in comparison.

Nuttall, Kevin's lawyer, asked her to describe Kevin's childhood. Joanne said that her older son had had an anger management problem since he was very young and that he had a great deal of trouble with school, attending 10 different schools and failing both eighth and ninth grades. The problem, as she saw it, was his reluctance to do his homework. "I tried everything I could so that he would finish his projects," she said, clearly exasperated.

She spoke of the incident in which he left a note saying "die bitch" for his ex-girlfriend, Katie, and threatened several other students and teachers at his school. Joanne recalled for the court that Kevin had pleaded guilty to two counts of communicating death threats.

After that, she, Ralston and Kevin went to see a youth counselor. "I told him that Kevin is not active, that he won't go out," she testified. "He just sits in front of the computer."

"Do you recall Ralston saying that Kevin was a lazy ass?" Nuttall asked.

"I don't know if he ever said that."

"Did you say that Kevin needed to feel like he meant something to someone?"

"Yeah."

She agreed that she had told police he had become increasingly withdrawn from the family starting two years before the homicide—about the same time his grandmother, with whom he was close, died. "He spent more time with his friends," she said. "He didn't want to go to certain places with us." He had an increasingly difficult relationship with his stepfather, and she was compelled to take over all his disciplining, she said.

When asked if she had ever seen Ralston abuse Kevin, she said she only recalled her son telling her of one incident of the stepfather beating the boy with a plastic baseball bat, but she hadn't seen it herself. But she acknowledged that in family counseling her son had accused her of failing to protect him from the stepfather.

"Do you recall that you and [your husband] were emotional and apologetic?" Nuttall asked.

"Of course," she said.

* * *

It was the second week of February when Nuttall presented his final argument on Kevin's behalf. Since Kevin had already admitted to killing Johnathon, the only way to get Kevin off would be to hope that the jury accepted the idea that Kevin was not responsible for his actions when he was suffering from the effects of intermittent explosive disorder.

"I know it sounds gruesome," Nuttall said. "But the best defense of Kevin is the attack itself." He paused and then continued. "The explosion and the animalistic fury demonstrated by 71 stab wounds to the body, to the head, to the hands—hacks, slices," he told them. "If that is not emotion out of control, I don't know what else it is."

He told them that as horrifying as Johnathon's death was, Kevin wasn't truly responsible because of his overwhelming psychological problems. "What we have here is a monstrous act, but an act not committed by a monster." He asked the jury to consider the crime as manslaughter, rather than first-degree murder.

He asked them to consider the difficulties Kevin had faced in life, what he described as a "dysfunctional life in a dysfunctional family." He was 16, failing in school yet again, lived with a neglectful mother and an abusive stepfather who both clearly favored his little brother.

Nuttall pointed out that Kevin woke up angry that day and it was made worse by having his friends over. Their pointless destruction only served to stir up Kevin's anger, which many acknowledged he had a very hard time controlling.

He then surprised many in the courtroom by putting at least part of the blame for Johnathon's death on Ashley. Nuttall asserted that when she did nothing to dissuade them from their announced plan to kill Kevin's entire family, she was giving it her approval. "On its face,

Ashley is guilty of aiding and abetting a homicide," he said. "But we don't hold her to that, because she couldn't have known that Kevin's anger would erupt 45 minutes later."

The court was still in stunned silence when McCaskill made his appeal on Tim's behalf. He pointed out that there was no evidence or testimony that indicated Tim had harmed Johnathon or helped Kevin to do so.

All he was guilty of was trying to impress his girlfriend with a stupid story—which they admitted he had done before. He was sure that he could win her back by convincing her he was a vampire, and the other boys played along. "There was no plan here," McCaskill said. "This is an improvisation." The only problem was that Kevin—who he called "a ticking time-bomb"—acted on it.

Then it was Lenzin's turn to speak for Pierre. He pointed out that both other boys testified that Pierre—who he described as "shy" and "non-confrontational"—was in the living room at the time of the killing and didn't not take part in the disposal of Johnathon's body. He was, in fact, the only one without a speck of Johnathon's blood on him or his clothes. "The reason is . . .," the lawyer said, pausing for effect. " . . . he was not involved."

Pierre went along with the murder plot on the phone call to Ashley, Lenzin allowed, only because he was helping his friend try to win back his girlfriend. Even so, he asserted, the tape showed that Pierre's part of the phone call was "minimal" and "unenthusiastic," compared to what Tim and Kevin had said.

After he was done, both Nuttall and Lenzin addressed the attempted murder charge leveled at their clients after the melee with Ralston by claiming that the stepfather actually attacked Kevin, who was defending himself, and that Pierre only stepped in to try to protect his friend from a stepfather he knew had abused Kevin in the past.

* * *

The following day, Goody presented the jury with an entirely different scenario. Reminding the court that Dr. Wood's investigations led him to conclude that the meat cleaver—and not just the green-handled kitchen knife or black-handled hunting knife—was part of the attack on Johnathon, he surmised that at least two of the boys were involved in the killing. "This common-sense conclusion, ladies and gentlemen, immediately undermines, indeed destroys" the defense's claim that Kevin, in a fit of rage, was the sole killer.

He pointed out that all three boys took part in the phone call to Ashley—which they did not know that she was taping—and that each of them separately boasted that they were going to kill that day. "It may not have been a complicated plan," Goody said. "But it was a plan." And events unfolded according to that plan. Johnathon was the first of Kevin's family to come home and he was brutally murdered. Ralston came home next and he too was attacked—by both Kevin and Pierre—but he survived to call the police. If he hadn't, events could have turned out quite differently.

As for Bourget's diagnosis of the Intermittent Explosive Disorder that threw Kevin into such an uncontrollable, animalistic fury, Goody pointed out that the doctor only had Kevin's word to go by and that much of his testimony was at odds with other evidence. And, he said, even Bourget herself considered Kevin's claim that the call and Johnathon's murder happening on the same day was a "coincidence" to be preposterous.

Next, Goody assailed Nuttall's claim that the nature of the attack indicated that Kevin did not premeditate the crime. He even called it the "defense's undoing."

Goody explained that of the 71 sharp-force wounds Johnathon suffered that day, only the last three—including the one that severed his windpipe—were life-threatening. The others, he said, were generally superficial and much more measured, as though the assailant or assailants sadistically intended to cause him the maximum amount of suffering possible before finally finishing him off. "They were calculated to cause harm and pain, but not death." Those first 68 slashes, hacks and stabs, he said, certainly would not have come from a 250-pound assailant—whom the defense characterized as a "raging bull"—in an uncontrolled fit of pure passion. Instead, he hypothesized, Kevin finally slashed Johnathon's throat "because he had decided it was time for his younger brother to die, completing the first phase of the plan to kill his family." The same plan the boys had detailed to Ashley less than an hour earlier.

Goody asked the jury to consider the taped conversation once again, especially how freely and easily the boys talked about the plan to murder Kevin's family. He told them that "it flowed completely naturally" because it was a real plan, not some fantasy made up just to impress Ashley.

Goody also reminded the court of how the boys had ransacked the house, not just making a terrible mess and damaging property, but stealing cash, identification and credit cards, which they intended to use. Why would they have done this with Ralston expected home at any minute, unless "he was not going to remain alive to tell anyone?"

After he finished, Justice Watt charged the jury to come up with a verdict. He reminded them that they were only to decide on the guilt of the boys in reference to the first-degree murder charge in the death of Johnathon and the attempted murder charge against Kevin and Pierre resulting from the attack on Ralston. And he warned them not to let the boys' self-centered personalities and disregard for the property of others influence their decision.

* * *

After the jury left, Watt heard from one more witness. Sarah (not her real name) is the mother of Sean, Johnathon's best friend. She knew Johnathon very well and noticed that he was acting a bit stranger than usual about ten days before he was killed. When she asked what was wrong, he said he was worried about his mother. "He said, 'She's been having a really hard time with my brother,'" Sarah told the court.

She knew that Kevin had been doing very poorly in school, so she told Johnathon that being a teenager is tough and that he'd grow out of the phase he was in. She assured Johnathon that his big brother loved him.

"No, he hates me," Johnathon told her. "He thinks he's the devil . . . he wants to kill me.'"

She assumed that Kevin and he had had a fight and it had gotten a bit rough for the younger, much smaller brother. She did her best to convince him that his brother didn't want to harm him.

His response shocked her. Johnathon looked at her, she testified, and said: "You don't know my brother, he's evil."

CHAPTER 6

# the truth about pretty girls

Reporter Joseph Brean was not disappointed by the trial. He'd never covered a murder case before, and this one was a classic. It had young love, sibling rivalry, the Internet and vampires. In various ways, it pitted rich against poor, black against white and children against their parents. It featured a star witness so attractive and composed that she looked like she'd just walked off a movie set, who took it upon herself to try to save the day after three brutish, self-interested young thugs bragged about plans to kill an entire family and to take out their violent frustrations on the public at large. If ever there was a case where a young reporter could make a name for himself, this was it.

As an added bonus, Brean was huddling with some of the best in the business. He was covering the case for the *National Post,* and that put him in a group with Vivian Song from *The Toronto Sun*, Peter Small from *The Toronto Star* and Christie Blatchford from *The Globe & Mail.* Brean did his best to learn from them all and was particularly impressed with Blatchford, whose work he had read for years and always appreciated. That they were all friendly and helpful to a young reporter like him was a pleasant surprise.

But not everyone was as gracious. Many people involved with the case made it obvious they considered Brean the last reporter in line when they were giving out information. Not only was he young—in his late twenties—but his inexperience with the court process and the people involved sometimes showed.

And he worked for the *Post*. Although the *Post* is an influential paper, especially when it comes to business, there are some people in Toronto who consider it something like the foreign press, even though it's based in suburban Toronto. The *Post* is new to the scene, having been founded in 1998, and drew much ire from the Toronto establishment in its infancy because much-reviled media baron Conrad Black said he started it as a conservative voice to counter what he saw as the liberal bias of the *Star* and the *Globe*. Even the *Sun* was insulted, as they considered the *Post*'s job description already filled by their sometimes outrageous tabloid.

To do the job well, Brean realized he would have to work harder and to be more innovative than the others. One of the first things he did was get to know Ashley. She was clearly the key to understanding the case. Without her, it was nothing more than three pointless thugs sitting around a house until one went crazy and shredded his little brother. Ashley, the beautiful rich girl mixed up with them, was what made the case interesting. She added drama, intrigue and sex appeal. And he wasn't the only one who thought so. After Ashley's testimony, Blatchford wrote that she had "impeccable instincts, an unwavering sense of what is right and the courage to act," and, in her column, called Ashley "a force for goodness."

Brean saw his break one day when he was standing behind Ashley in line at the court's coffee shop. She was fumbling for change, so he told the cashier he'd pay for her Coke along with his coffee. Ashley accepted, turned to thank Brean and flashed him a warm, welcoming smile.

After that initial meeting, Brean made an effort to talk with Ashley every day. They became friends of a sort and Brean did his best to keep the conversation light. He scored some points with her when he nicknamed her "Jackpot," a reference to a remark by Tim's lawyer, David McCaskill, who said that Tim had "hit the jackpot" when a girl so obviously superior to him agreed to go out with him. They talked about some of the things they had in common—Brean had grown up in the same area as Ashley and had even taken the same city bus to school, although about a decade earlier. He would bring up Tim and she would sigh and complain about him, often pointing out which parts of his testimony she claimed were "bullshit."

The pair became so close that some parties close to the trial began to jokingly accuse Brean of "coming on" to the girl, and the other reporters even started calling her his "little girlfriend." It didn't bother him. Now his youth was working for him, rather than against him. His good looks didn't hurt, either. And he was finding out things from her that nobody else could.

When her testimony was finished, Ashley came by to say good-bye to Brean. She told him that she was going to Quebec on a ski vacation and that she wouldn't come back until after the verdict. He wished her well and promised to keep her up to date on the case.

After she left, something about her stuck with Brean. In an attempt to prove that she was into the same vampire fantasies as Tim and that she actually would have been impressed by his plan to murder and his offer of human blood, McCaskill had asked her why her e-mail address was biteforblood@hotmail.com. It seemed less like the kind of name a sweet, innocent girl like she seemed to be on the stand would pick and more like the kind of name preferred by someone like Tim. Since all of the testimony up until that point had indicated that Kevin, and Kevin alone, killed Johnathon, the only real tie Tim and Pierre had to the murder was the telephone call. If he could prove that Ashley was the kind of girl who could be wooed by promises of mass murder and offers of human blood to drink, maybe he could convince the jury that the call really was just a coincidence. That Tim and Pierre were nothing but big talkers, unaware that their friend Kevin was actually taking everything they said quite seriously.

But it became something of a non-event at the time. Ashley told the court the e-mail address was inspired by the name of a local band she liked. It didn't mean anything to her and the court appeared to accept it as just another example of Ashley finding herself in the middle of a place and time in which silly young men like to use the concept of pretend violence to show how cool they are.

But Brean couldn't stop thinking about it. He remembered talking with Ashley about Tim's testimony that he drank her blood after she cut herself and that she said that it totally grossed her out. She was pretty vehement about it. So why would a girl dead set against drinking blood call herself "biteforblood" on the Internet? Brean knew that e-mail addresses are a key part of a teenager's identity and that they often go to agonizing lengths to pick the perfect one. Surely someone as intelligent and well read as Ashley could come up with something more creative (and more accurate) than "biteforblood." They must have been one hell of a band.

Brean decided to Google the name to find out what was so special about these guys. Every band has a website or at least a MySpace page these days, he figured. To his surprise, no such band existed, but what he found was far more fascinating.

An account on VampireFreaks.com under the name "Biteforblood," which gave biteforblood@hotmail.com as its owner's e-mail contact address came up on his searches repeatedly. He looked at the user profile and the physical self-description confirmed it was Ashley's account. He looked down to see her likes. Among them, he spotted: Blood, pain, hating people, darkness, thunder, fire, drugs, cemeteries, knives and guys with sexy longish black hair and green eyes. At the bottom of her profile, she listed sanguinarius.com, a now-defunct website dedicated to the drinking of human blood, as one of her favorite sites. On her profile page at Xanga.com, another social networking site popular with teenagers, she wrote: "I like to wear a lot of black and like a lot of dark. Blood is good . . . both flowing and . . . Yum."

She had a blog on VampireFreaks and another on Xanga. Brean realized he had to read them. All 15,000 words of them.

He found that they were not focused on blood and gore. She didn't write like a typical Goth kid, using big words with little care about their meaning and overcomplicated syntax. Actually, he found, she had some genuine writing talent. For the most part, they were the typical writings of an advantaged—maybe a bit spoiled—teenager. She wrote about her friends, her job at Lick's Homeburgers, school and boyfriends. She complained about her mother, her workload at school, how perfidious boyfriends could be and her disdain for her psychiatrist visits. She also wrote about how "hot" certain guys were. In all her writing, she showed an impressive ego, a sometimes charming sense of humor and a desire to play with language.

Brean read it all and noticed significant edits and a bit of a change in language after July 22, 2004. Her blog that day began, "Well my mom reads this, hey mom, thanks for reading this. Her excuse is it's public, so are the bathrooms in the park, but you don't use them."

There was only one, oblique reference to Johnathon's murder. Many people who use social networking sites fill in long questionnaires in an effort to give their readers a little better insight into their personality. In one rather exhaustive one, Ashley answers the question "When have you cried the most?" by writing: "It's a three way tie between when I thought Will was dead, when we broke up and the whole . . . November thing." On the same quiz, she claimed to have "hundreds" of scars and that she lied "constantly, though I'm bad at it."

And, to Brean's surprise, she wrote about the trial. She even mentioned him once, calling him a "really hott reporter" and musing that he was "hitting on" her.

Most of what she wrote about the trial consisted of complaints about how much time it was taking out of her life, how much school she was missing, how slow the process was and the numerous delays (including one because a "stupid jurer" got sick).

But a couple of things stood out for Brean. The first was her vehement desire for her parents not to show up in court during her testimony. She wrote:

> Got in a huge fight with my parents last night. I don't want them coming in the courtroom with me when I testify (If I didn't say it somewhere else, court is on thursday/friday) because . . . I don't even know why . . . It's just one of those things . . . They think I'm hiding something from them or that I don't trust them, and neither of which is the case. Well . . . I sort of don't trust them, but only the way every teen doesn't really trust their parents. Anyway, it's like . . . When I'm performing, singing or dancing or whatever, I never want them there, it makes me nervous, but then they asked how could I have my friends there . . . I don't even understand why I feel like this I just do, and I don't want them being there to jeopardize my testimony. . . .

Brean remembered that her parents had not been present when she testified. It wasn't too surprising, actually. Despite her complaining about her mother's intrusions, Ashley rarely had any trouble getting her way at home. One figure key in the case described her parents as a "couple of old hippies," and said "she could do no wrong in their eyes" and that she was "the tail that wagged that dog." Other sources also indicated that if Ashley wanted something badly enough, neither parent would put up much of a fight.

While doing a good job on the stand was understandably important to Ashley, it was mystifying as to how her parents would jeopardize that. And why did she refer to it as "performing?"

The blog continued: "... if I screw up and those fuck holes get off with a day less than they deserve I'll blame myself and never forgive myself."

It was clear she wanted to see Tim, Kevin and Pierre suffer, but unclear as to whether it was for murdering Johnathon or for dragging her into it.

When she finally gave her testimony, she was relieved that it went well, but clearly annoyed with the cross-examination style of Tim's lawyer, David McCaskill, who she called "Bigasskill." She wrote:

> Thank god! It's finally over!!!! Well . . . not entirely, but I'm done on the stand. TOOK THEM FRICKEN LONG ENOUGH! Johnathon's mother and aunt came and thanked me and said I was their hero and what an amazing thing we did. It makes me sound like an ass. Mr. Bigasskill (hahaha B. you're terrible) was such a douche. I wanted to smack him so fucking hard.

But everyone who watched her in court—other than Tim—had nothing but praise for her performance. She thought that was funny:

> So there is this really hott reporter and he was hitting on me today which was fun for me. Also Christie Blatchford (another reporter for the Globe) is in love with me. Honestly, she called me "regal". ME. REGAL./ Bwahaha.

And, just before she left for her Quebec ski trip, Ashley left a couple of interesting comments, revealing her attitude toward Tim, who she (illegally) mentioned by name. In the first, she accuses Tim of perjury:

> Well, Tim said a bunch of bull shit and it was hilarious. He's not done yet so i get to back Monday and Tuesday (at least) to watch more riddiculous lies. I can't wait!

And in her final trial-related post, she wrote:

> Another day in court. It was much more entertaining today because the Crown lawyer caught Tim in a whole web of lies. he almost had a panick attack. It was like a car crash, terrible but you can't look away. You almost feel sorry for him . . . No.

And later in the same posting, she seems confident Tim will be found guilty and end up in prison. She wrote: "I'm done, it's shower time. Bwahaha, but I don't have to be afraid to drop the soap, unlike tim, sucka."

Brean could hardly believe what he'd found. After those initial successes, he "Googled the hell out of her." He searched not just her name and onscreen nickname, but the names and nicknames of her friends and some of her frequently used phrases like "bwahaha" and "anysnitch." When he was satisfied that he could find no more information on his laptop, he went to the *Post* and used a bigger, more capable computer.

Overloaded with this sensitive information, he didn't know what to do. Even though it was his first murder trial, he was aware that it was considered bad form to publish anything the jury hadn't already seen. He was sure he'd be found in contempt. But he couldn't leave it alone and he wrote his article anyway. When he was finished, he ran it by his boss, Steve Murray, who told him to run with it. Brean did, changing the names and nicknames just enough to ensure Ashley's identity wouldn't be uncovered.

* * *

At court the next day, Feb. 15, 2005, Brean was surprised to see that the lawyers treated him no differently than they had the day before. Blatchford and Small, on the other hand, were shocked and impressed with his story and told him so. They particularly liked the inclusion of "Bigasskill," even though McCaskill was far from overweight. The merriment it brought helped ease the boredom of another day waiting for the jury to come to a conclusion.

With nothing else to do, Brean and Blatchford decided to teach Small how to play gin rummy at about 5:15 that afternoon. They had just started the lesson on a courthouse hallway floor when McCaskill walked by. Thinking he might appreciate his new nickname, Blatchford handed him a copy of the *Post*, which had Brean's story on the front page.

As he read, McCaskill's mood changed from jovial to deadly serious. He looked at Brean, told him there would be some "legal issues" with the piece and headed upstairs to confer with Lenzin and Nuttall.

Alarmed and sure that he would be held in contempt, Brean excused himself from the other reporters and headed to the men's room. He was just leaving a urinal when he was immediately surrounded by three big men in black robes. Lenzin—with his long red hair, the most fearsome-looking of the trio—asked him where he got the information he put in the piece. Brean told him the Internet. Lenzin rolled his eyes. It was clear he didn't put a lot of faith in the information superhighway. Lenzin asked for his notes. Brean said that he could lay his hands on some, but most of them were on his computer. Trying to be helpful, he told Lenzin that he could get most of the information by Googleing Ashley.

To his surprise, they did. Although the lawyers managed to find Ashley's VampireFreaks page and her Xanga blog, she had recently removed much of what she had written. Brean surmised that she had been warned by her host that her blog was attracting extra traffic from him and his editors. They looked at what was on the Net and his story again, and recommended he get himself a lawyer.

Brean returned to the press pack while calling the *Post* to see if they could get him a lawyer. As he hung up, relieved that they promised to take care of him, he could tell from the other reporters that he had transformed from reporter observing the case to part of the case itself.

He was talking with Blatchford and Small when the trio of defense lawyers passed by and went into the courtroom. Lenzin had Brean's article in his hand. The entire press horde, including Brean, followed them in. To their amazement, they didn't argue for contempt charges against Brean, but perjury against Ashley. They wanted the jury to stop deliberating. They wanted to call Ashley back to the stand. They even mulled over the idea of Brean taking the stand.

Watt asked for the article. He skimmed it and asked the collected defense lawyers how they could have missed such a thing. Lenzin said that he had done an Internet search on Ashley (using Yahoo, not Google) and had found nothing out of the ordinary. Watt asked how Brean had been able to, then. Lenzin replied that the blog was: "hidden within this technical thing called the Internet, and I don't know how he could have found it." Wrong answer.

Watt told the court he would read the article over the dinner break and address the matter at 8:30.

When Watt came back, he was fuming. Brean later wrote: "New evidence was not supposed to come out in the newspapers before it was presented to the court, especially not while the jury was deliberating." Watt sighed and told the lawyers and press: "If this young woman did not commit perjury, she came close enough for government work to it. And I just don't understand what else I can realistically do. I don't see in this case how Humpty can be put back together again."

When the jury came in, Brean said he could tell they knew something was wrong. Once they were seated, Watt thanked them for their great sacrifice over these last four months and told them that they could go home.

After countless hours of heart-wrenching testimony and over $1 million in public money spent, the Johnathon Madden murder trial had ended in a mistrial.

At least two reliable sources later told me that jurors told them that they were very close to finding all three boys guilty when the trial ended.

A new trial date was set for November 14, 2005—almost two years after Johnathon's death.

CHAPTER 7

# starting over

Ashley's wasn't the only blog Joseph Brean found when he started combing the Internet for information related to the case. While searching for information about Kevin, he came across a blog entry called "My Ex-Best Friend is a Murderer." It read:

> I get home today and my friend who had just gotten out of jail (No, I don't hang out with a bad crowd, I'm a loner I hang out with no crowd :P.) pasted me a link from cp24, first thing I assumed was that it had something to do with My Ex-Best friend murdering his brother Johnathan. So i clicked the link and a few minutes later he supplied me with more links with extended stories on the court hearing, I mean there's not much to say about it, I wasn't there when he did it. I did know the guy for years though and we were good buds up until his girlfriend dumped him for me(woops) So I hope now he gets a life sentence cause I know if he gets free he's going to come and kill me, seriously. I'm just going to post the links to the news stories; I don't really feel like talking much on the subject, the guys dead to me.

He didn't post anything illegal. Although he did try to identify Johnathon, he misspelled his name "Johnathan," which is not far from the name "Jonathan" that the media had been using to describe the case.

But, on an Internet discussion forum, the same person, let's call him Alex, posted the names of all three accused. Since they were all under 18, that was against the law, although the media was briefly allowed to publish the names of Kevin and Tim while they were at large overnight in and around Taylor Creek Park. But then they were identified as missing persons, not suspects in a murder case. Alex wrote:

> I was asked by a member here to reveal the names, and I will because I hate that fucking Youth Protection bullshit. I would testify against Kevin Madden because some of you don't understand how disgusting this is . . . im sorry, even if I had a lifetime friendship with him I would wish death upon him.

Alex didn't go to the police or lawyers, he said, because he didn't believe in the legal process. But he didn't mind talking to the media. He did an anonymous interview with Citytv and, when Brean contacted him, he was more than happy to talk via e-mail. But he had one—somewhat hypocritical—condition, he didn't want his name to appear in the paper. Brean agreed.

Alex told Brean that he'd known Kevin for about 10 years and had gone to his house many times, mostly to play video games. He said he had witnessed several fights between Kevin and Ralston, but chalked them up to youthful rebellion. He also spoke about Kevin's disdain for Johnathon. "I know he was really annoyed by his little brother a lot," he wrote. "But a lot of people can't stand younger siblings, so that wasn't anything out of the ordinary either." Alex described Kevin's life as being fraught with discord, hatred and violence, a situation he considered perfectly normal.

Brean asked why they were no longer friends. Alex boasted that Kevin's girlfriend dumped him, so that she could date Alex instead. The girl in question was Katie, the one Kevin pleaded guilty to threatening with his "die, bitch" note. Alex said that he'd heard Kevin had been depressed ever since.

If they weren't talking, Brean asked Alex how he knew that. They had a friend in common, Alex told him. If Brean really wanted to know about Kevin, he said, he should get in touch with his friend Gabriel. Kevin and he had become practically inseparable since Katie left him. Alex gave Brean Gabriel's e-mail address.

Brean sent Gabriel an e-mail asking if he wanted to talk about Kevin. What he got back surprised him. Gabriel wrote back a long, rambling essay about how he taught Kevin the "truths of Nazism." In it, Gabriel likened himself to Edward Norton's handsome, charismatic and intelligent character from the film *American History X*, and he compared Kevin to the obese, mentally challenged character with a hair-trigger violent side played by Ethan Suplee in the same film. While he may have been a fan of the film to the point of fantasy, he had clearly missed its obviously anti-Nazi point.

And that wasn't the only thing he seemed to have missed. Gabriel's message was written in a style that, to be kind, would embarrass most fourth graders. Sprinkled with multi-syllable words he clearly didn't know the meaning of, the message was couched in a bizarrely stilted, almost unfathomable perversion of English:

> To speak the tale of Kevin would oblige me to state the significance of my life, and thus I shall attempt to do so. The essence of death entails inquirer, as the life remains excused, I question some time if the life ever existed. Kevin was folly to the vanity of knowledge and life. Kevin was bewildered and beguiled by the only structure and religion he had ever acquired, society. His life was a perpetual misery, caused by reconciliation of eternal vanity. Though I feel obliged to elucidate, as I shall . . .

Gabriel claimed to have known Kevin since they were very young children and to have noticed early on that he was different from the other children. "Essentially he could manipulate perception; he could induce accentuated states of comprehension, such as indulging in toy activities," he wrote. "As most children would irrelevantly occupy their time playing with toys, Kevin would contrive intricate and unfathomably zany scenarios." This apparently meant that while the other kids in class were having fun with toys, Kevin played by himself.

Gabriel did offer some tortuously worded insight on Kevin's development and home life. He had very little respect for Kevin's parents, writing:

> Kevin was by nature afraid, thus hostile. This I assume derived from the neglect he endured as a child. Kevin's father abandoned him on Christmas Eve, when Kevin was five. His mother hysterically lost, married an ex-convict. And thus the new stepfather

> assumed responsibility for Kevin and his brother. . . . Kevin would frequently tell me how his stepfather would favor Jonathon for mysterious purposes, and as yet beat Kevin as a youth.

Later, he added: "With the inconclusive beatings from his step father, and Kevin's now obscured personality incited ridicule from school, and thus the anger grew."

But while Gabriel was appalled at Kevin's stories about Ralston that were perhaps fanciful, he considered Kevin's torture of Johnathon to be par for the course:

> Surely they had a violent relationship. I can vividly recollect Kevin venturing home from school in grade 6, only to encounter his brother passively watching television. Kevin then forcefully smashed his brother's head against a solid wooden chair. Then grasped the heels of his brother and whorled him almost majestically in circles. Then to let go and watch his 90 lbs brother collide with the wall. Though it was peculiar, despite such unprovoked occurences of irrelevant violence, Kevin never spoke of his brother in any manner.

Then Gabriel began to portray himself as a teacher molding the unformed personality of his friend. Looking to channel his "cognitive hate," Gabriel introduced Kevin to "National Socialism"—Nazism. Whether his teachings inspired it or not, Gabriel noted that Kevin espoused a racist philosophy:

> With his father being black this further complicated family life. To which I now assume begun the most atrocious moments of Kevin's life. Upon venturing to school after being beaten at home, he would frequently engage in fights with all students. Even when the vast forces of blacks encumbered me, Kevin would stand prominently and mutter racial provocative slurs.

Gabriel said that although Kevin claimed to be a Goth, "it was merely an instrument to shield his fear." He went on to blame Kevin's hatreds on the fire (which wiped out Kevin's beloved collection of Tom Clancy books), Katie (who Gabriel incorrectly said had had him thrown in jail), his "stepfather a black ex convict" and society in general. These factors, along with his own guidance, he said, drove Kevin to Nazism.

In the six months or so after the fire, Kevin would visit Gabriel and listen to his lectures about "the beauties of death" and other ideas he had.

Then Gabriel's e-mail addressed the murder:

> Now as for Kevin's two associates, Pierre and Tim. I was vaguely acquainted with them, they were more so substitutes for myself. I suppose Kevin felt I had progressed beyond ignorant hatred and devolved my own intellectual beliefs. Thus Kevin and I spoke on a time-to-time basis. satisfied with my prodigy Kevin, i revised my beliefs and continued to incline intellectually. Though I now realize it was to late for him. With his uncouth mother, his abusive step[father], his mentally challenged brother, Kevin could not endure. And so he rejected the system fucking him. He said no, i will not let life lie to me. I will not be encumbered by beliefs, motives and emotions I forbid. And with this contempt Kevin acted, and thus his brother he demised.

He closed with a recollection of the last time he had seen the boy he believed was his protégé. About two weeks before Johnathon's death, Kevin called Gabriel and asked him to help him pick out a knife. They went downtown together and Gabriel recommended that Kevin buy a small Swiss Army-style knife, which was not connected with Johnathon's death.

Aware that he had once again uncovered relevant evidence, Brean wrote a story about Kevin's Nazi past for the *Post*. It didn't run.

When Detective Sergeant Terry Wark, head of the murder investigation, found out about Gabriel, he interviewed him. He wasn't impressed. Neither, apparently, was Hank Goody, head of the prosecution, because Gabriel never spoke in or was mentioned in court. I asked Wark, an intelligent man of few, impeccably chosen words, why not.

"Guy was a total wing nut," he said.

* * *

David McCaskill quit as Tim's lawyer. In fact, he left criminal law altogether and took a job with the Ontario Ministry of Labour. In his place,

John Dennis filed a bid for bail on Tim's behalf. David North, working with Dennis Lenzin on Pierre's defense, also filed for his client.

At a hearing on July 8, 2005, the details of the crime and the involvement of Tim and Pierre were presented before Superior Court Judge Mary Lou Benotto, and Dennis could tell which way things were going. He withdrew Tim's request. North held on until the end. Benotto denied Pierre bail.

* * *

The second trial began November 15, 2005, when a new judge, Justice David McCombs, told 230 prospective jurors not to be influenced by the fact that the first trial ended in a mistrial.

About three weeks later, the first witness took the stand. It was Ashley, and she was under a very different kind of scrutiny than the last time.

She told her story much as she had the first time, but without as much flair. Her parents were not present. Ashley admitted that she had gone out with Tim, but was trying to dump him.

Goody asked why she was trying to break off their relationship.

Ashley replied that Tim had told her that he killed people in the Don Valley and drank their blood.

Goody asked her how that made her feel.

She said she was "weirded out."

She testified that Tim called her on November 25, 2003 from Kevin's house and told her of a murder plot. She was so distraught that she asked her friends for help, ignoring her parents and the police. She and her friends then taped a second call in which Tim, Pierre and Kevin—to varying degrees—boasted that they would kill Kevin's family. Her friends then called police, gave them the tape and she found out Johnathon was dead later that night.

Goody played the tape to a hushed jury.

But under cross-examination, John Dennis, Tim's new lawyer, introduced Ashley's online persona of Biteforblood. He asked her to confirm that it was the name of her profile at VampireFreaks.com and that she posted semi-nude photos of herself on the site and expressed an interest in "blood" and "pain." She acknowledged that it was hers.

He asked her if she had posted "Blood is good . . . both flowing and . . . yum" on her profile at Xanga.com. She admitted that she had.

Dennis asked her why she had picked the name "Biteforblood." She said she knew of a band with that name and it sounded cool.

"You disagree you employed the term 'biteforblood' because of an interest in vampirism?" he asked her.

"Yes, I disagree with you," she answered.

Nobody called her a "force for goodness" that day.

* * *

After the rest of the witnesses, including Ralston, delivered pretty much the same testimony they had in the first trial, Nuttall delivered his closing argument on Kevin's behalf on February 17. As in the previous trial, he admitted that Kevin, and Kevin alone, killed Johnathon. And again he argued that the appropriate charge should be manslaughter, not murder, because the stabbing wasn't planned, but had occurred during a fit of rage. "Kevin went berserk," he told the jury. And, as before, he indicated that the ferocity of the attack proved his hypothesis. "The act speaks for itself," he lawyer said. "He went on and on and on stabbing him."

As for the attack on Ralston, Nuttall attributed it to "ongoing tensions" between the two of them, which he said "sparked a fight." If he had planned to kill his stepfather, as the Crown claimed, why didn't he use one of the knives or the meat cleaver, both of which were handy, instead of his fists?

Goody asked the jury to remember the tape. He reminded them that Kevin had told Ashley that he had planned to kill his entire family one by one as they returned home. When Johnathon got home, Kevin almost immediately murdered him. And when Ralston came in later, Kevin attacked him quickly, with intent to kill. "He said exactly what he was planning and intended to do," Goody said. He also told them that Kevin's being diagnosed with Intermittent Explosive Disorder did nothing to change that.

Dennis and Lenzin argued that Tim and Pierre were nothing more than witnesses to Kevin's fit of rage. The call, they said, was simply Tim's only way to try to win Ashley back. He was a young man in love; he was desperate. She was so much prettier, richer, more popular and intelligent than him, he knew he had to work hard. He decided to appeal to the one thing he knew she loved—blood—and offered it to her. Of course, these were just idle boasts, like his claims of murdering passersby in the Don Valley. He had no idea Kevin would actually go through with it.

As for Pierre, he was simply going along for the ride. He was trying to help his new buddy Tim get back in good standing with his obviously kinky girlfriend.

Goody argued that the call and the attacks were just too much of a coincidence. Clearly, they had cooked up a plan to murder Kevin's family, and he had gone through with it. "All were in the house, together, waiting," he reminded them, and all three, he argued, were guilty.

* * *

On the fifth day of deliberations—February 28, 2006—the jury had come to a decision. The three young men rose as the jurors filed in. The foreman read the verdict. Kevin was found guilty of first-degree murder in the death of Johnathon and guilty in the charge of attempted murder against Ralston. Tim was guilty of manslaughter in the death of Johnathon. Pierre was found not guilty in the death of Johnathon and not guilty of the attempted murder of Ralston.

The courtroom was silent until McCombs looked at Pierre and told him: "You are free to leave the box." Stunned, Pierre walked away from the box, past the swinging door into the gallery and then ran into the arms of his mother, father and brother.

Tim began to cry as the court officers handcuffed him and Kevin, preparing to take them away again. Joanne could be heard crying as well while Kevin and Tim were led out of the room.

Outside the court, Pierre and his family rushed into a waiting minivan and left. They didn't make any comment to the herd of reporters who had followed them out. Instead, Lenzin spoke on their behalf.

He thanked the jury for their wise decision. "The only way I can interpret this verdict is that the jury came to the conclusion that that phone call did not indicate a serious plan," he said. Beaming, he told *The Toronto Star's* Peter Small, "I have never in my life been so pleased to reunite a young man with his family."

When Small asked him why the family had left so quickly and without comment, Lenzin replied, "I think he wants to sit down with his mom and dad and eat something other than institution food."

After conferring with his client, John Dennis came out to the street to tell reporters that, despite the streams of tears running down his face, Tim was happy with the verdict. "His emotions have always been very close to the surface during this whole trial," he said, adding that watching Kevin kill his little brother "traumatized" Tim and that he felt deep remorse throughout the trial. Dennis summed up Tim's actions in the killing by saying, "He was at the wrong place at the wrong time." When asked why his client received a manslaughter conviction despite the fact Kevin had admitted to being solely responsible for the killing, Dennis blamed it on the e-mail Tim sent Ashley in which he told her he gave Kevin the knife, although Tim had twice denied that particular detail in court.

Nuttall came out last and spoke for Kevin. He said that the jury found him "fully responsible" for Johnathon's death. When asked why he thought the jury did not take into account the Intermittent Explosive Disorder diagnosis, he said that they probably did, but must have felt that: "It wasn't sufficient rage to deprive him of the ability to attend what he was doing or plan and deliberate."

He also expressed a desire to see Kevin sentenced to a youth facility, so that he could have a chance to get the psychological help he needs.

Wark spoke for Joanne and Ralston. He said that this was just one point in a long and trying process that had taken a huge emotional toll on all of them, but especially Joanne. "She's lost two sons, one being the victim, one being the accused," he said. "God forbid that any one of us should be in that position." A reporter asked about Joanne's relationship with Kevin, noting that the two rarely even glanced at one another during either trial. Wark denied that she was ignoring Kevin. "She's still his mother," he reminded the media.

While Kevin's guilt was now clearly established, his sentence was anything but. If McCombs decided Kevin should be sentenced as an adult, the minimum sentence he would receive would be life in prison with no chance at parole for the first 10 years. But if he was deemed a young offender, the maximum he could receive would be six years in a juvenile facility and four in community supervision.

Michelle Mandel, a columnist for *The Toronto Sun*, later learned that the first thing Kevin did when he returned to Sprucedale was to go for a swim in the facility's pool. She surmised that he needed to calm his nerves.

CHAPTER 8

# big enough to know better?

It was May when the hearings to determine sentencing began. Crown Attorney Anna Tenhouse told the court that the drawings discovered in Kevin's backpack were a good indicator of how disturbed he really was. She described them as featuring "rather scary figures full of knives and using knives."

Nuttall countered that he considered the drawings to be "fairly benign" and explained that Kevin had made them at a troubled time before the murder in an effort to be accepted into an art school like his friend Pierre had been. He suggested that Kevin be given an opportunity to explain the drawings in court.

Justice McCombs disagreed. Instead, he wanted the drawings to be part of the evidence handed over to the psychiatric professionals who would be examining Kevin and Tim for the next month. He also took a moment to scold both teams for how long it had taken them to assemble their evidence for the sentencing round. McCombs reminded them of how emotional Joanne had been throughout the trial and that every moment it dragged on only made it more painful for her.

* * *

It was the beginning of September before Ian Swayze, a forensic psychiatrist from Toronto's Centre for Addiction and Mental Health, began to testify on his assessment of Kevin's psyche. The doctor had been before McCombs once before, in June, to ask for sufficient funding and resources to carry out the task. McCombs quickly agreed.

After the assessment, Swayze painted a very disturbing psychological portrait of Kevin—one somewhat at odds with the one Dominique Bourget had presented during the trial itself. He described the young man—now 19—as a "smoldering volcano" and said: "He has a serious and pervasive personality disorder. We are dealing with a gentleman who requires, really, a multiple therapeutic intervention over a protracted period of time."

Calling Kevin's "the most serious case, personally and professionally, that I have been involved with," Swayze described the teen as a "psychopath," which he explained is a person without "conscience, empathy and remorse." He said the condition is also "stubbornly resistant to treatment."

Tenhouse asked Swayze how much Kevin had progressed since killing his little brother almost three years ago.

"I would suggest that Kevin is likely very close to being the same individual as the day he was detained," he said. "So we are starting from square one."

The next witness was less strident in his opinion of Kevin's illness. Marc Levine, a counselor at the Sprucedale Youth Centre where Kevin was being held, testified that Kevin had actually shown him some remorse in custody, once telling him that Johnathon "didn't deserve to die because he was the most innocent in the family."

Nuttall then asked him if he thought Kevin was making any progress. Levine said that Kevin himself seemed to think so. When Levine asked him if he was a risk to the community, Kevin said, "By the time I am finished my sentence, I won't be." Levine also testified that Kevin expressed a desire to stay in the juvenile facility—rather than be sent to an adult prison—"in order to achieve his goals."

Under cross-examination, Swayze refuted what Levine gave as Kevin's self-description. When asked what he thought of what the counselor said about Kevin, he answered, "My first reaction is surprise, because it's different from my direct knowledge of him." He reiterated his opinion that Kevin was a psychopath, almost certainly incurable and absolutely without the ability to feel either guilt or remorse. Clearly, Swayze thought Kevin was playing Levine and that if he really believed him, Levine was making a dangerous mistake.

Nuttall then read the court a series of affidavits from Sprucedale employees who generally described Kevin as polite and co-operative in custody.

Swayze countered that he wasn't surprised at all. He said that psychopaths are often the best-behaved prisoners because they know how to manipulate people to get what they want. Kevin really wanted to stay in Sprucedale for six years, rather than face adult prison for at least 10 years and more likely the rest of his life, so Swayze said he was of the opinion that Kevin was affecting remorse to fool his keepers at Sprucedale into thinking he was making psychological progress.

When Levine was brought back to the stand, much of what he said backed up what Swayze had said. He said that Kevin had applied for an intensive behavioral rehabilitation program at Sprucedale, but was denied "because of his emotional detachment and general lack of remorse."

When asked his own opinion, Levine asserted that he felt Kevin was more suited to an adult prison than a youth facility. One of the reasons he gave was that he would be much older than most of the other inmates at any facility and that could make him liable to bully them.

When Swayze was asked his opinion of Tim, he said he should receive psychiatric treatment for two years in jail followed by at least three years of close supervision in the community. He described Tim as having made significant progress in custody, though he did once try to commit suicide by hanging himself.

Dennis asked Swayze what disorder Tim had. Swayze said he didn't know. Then, Dennis asked, how did he know what sentence was best to help him?

* * *

About a week later, McCombs heard the victim impact statements. The first to go was Joanne. She said:

> I really don't know where to start to explain the depth of my pain I have been feeling for the past 2 1/2 years. My two sons were the reason I enjoyed life.
>
> Kevin slowly began to withdraw from our family and stopped wanting to be involved in family activities and outings, not sure if that was due to his age or the passing of his Nana [grandmother].

It was very hard for me to watch him go through rough times and not be able to help him. It was very painful for me to see him be sad. I wish I had known how to get through to him.

I feel that everything inside me is dead. My sons were my pride and joy. There are times when I look outside and see the kids playing and laughing. It's so hard to swallow because I think that should have been my boys playing and laughing and enjoying life the way it was meant to be enjoyed.

You can lose people you love and think that's painful but the loss of your own child is the deepest painful gut-wrenching feeling that you can ever imagine.

I just feel lost. I miss my sons; I miss being a mother; I know I am still a mother but I feel I cannot enjoy life now like other mothers are doing. I feel like I have lost both my children.

And if love alone could have saved Johnathon he never would have died. In life I loved him dearly, in death I love him still; in my heart he holds a place that only a mother can feel. It broke my heart to lose him, but he didn't go alone for half my heart went with him. Every mother dreams for the best for their children and now I have to try and help my eldest son to get the help he needs and to help him recover from this tragedy because I love him, he is all I have left.

I will never forget what has happened, but I will work on forgiving him and I hope he will work on forgiving me for not knowing how to fix the problems of growing up and being a teenager, or not being there that fatal day, as maybe he would have talked to me.

If Johnathon were here now he would forgive his big brother. In Johnathon's eyes he was and will always be his big brother. I have to help my oldest son to get the help he needs to recover from this tragedy because I love him.

When she finished, she made a surprising request. She asked McCombs that if Kevin were to be judged an adult, the publication ban preventing the media from identifying Johnathon be removed. McCombs asked why.

"We have not been able to acknowledge Johnathon properly since his death," she replied. Joanne claimed that since the media storm that surrounded the trial, everyone had concentrated on Johnathon's death and seemed to have forgotten what he was like when he was alive. She said that if the ban was lifted, she would make a memorial website for Johnathon.

Ralston followed Joanne and spoke not about how he was attacked, but about how much Johnathon's death had affected him. "I have not been able to find any peace," he said. "Johnathon was a very special boy. He was a free spirit, a wanderer, and a compassionate, caring child."

He broke down as he told the court he did everything he could to keep the little boy safe. "But I feel that I failed because I could not keep my son safe in our own home," he said.

The last to speak was Kevin Madden Sr., the boys' biological father. He spoke not of missing Johnathon, but instead appealed to McCombs to keep Kevin Jr. out of adult prison. He said that he had visited him at the youth facility and that he was doing well there.

* * *

On the final day of testimony, Tim and Kevin were allowed to plead their own cases before sentencing. Tim went first. He reminded the court that he did not take an active part in Johnathon's killing, but instead watched in horror as Kevin hacked him to death.

Tim then offered Joanne his apologies, then said he wished the whole thing had never happened. "Although I only met Johnathon once or twice, I could tell he was a very sweet young boy and he didn't deserve what happened to him," Tim said. "And for me to have taken part in what happened that day, I'm very, very sorry."

Joanne burst into tears.

Goody recommended that Tim be sentenced as an adult, but spend the rest of his custody in Syl Apps. He asked the judge to sentence Tim to spend two more years in the facility—where he was receiving daily treatments—and another three years of supervision once he rejoins the community.

He called Tim an "underachieving youth," who was a "constant truant, petty thief and vandal." Tim idolized Kevin because he had the boldness Tim himself lacked. While he admitted the boy was "ultimately salvageable," he said that he was a long way from being a contributing member of society and wouldn't get anywhere unless he received professional treatment in an institutional facility.

Dennis countered by saying that Tim had no idea that Kevin was going to murder anyone the day he called Ashley. He said that Tim has long been "deeply ashamed of his cowardly behavior" in not doing anything to stop Kevin from killing his little brother.

"Mr. Ferriman didn't have the guts to step in and stop this when he could," David Harris, Dennis's co-counsel added. "Remember, though, that he was a 15-year-old at the time."

Dennis also pointed out that all reports indicated that Tim had made significant progress during his stay at Syl Apps. He asked McCombs to release Tim from the facility, but to continue his rehabilitation and supervision once outside.

Kevin waived his right to speak before the court.

Goody said that Kevin should be sent to an adult prison and that, if he should ever get out of prison, he should be under constant supervision. "The egregious nature of Kevin's behavior is of critical importance," he told McCombs, "because it informs us how seriously he is disturbed and how much he needs treatment."

He then reminded the court of Kevin's history of violence. He pointed out that both Swayze and Levine had testified to his psychopathic personality and that, despite what Kevin himself said, he had shown no genuine guilt or remorse for any of his crimes. Goody then warned that Kevin has a high likelihood to re-offend.

When given his chance to rebut, Nuttall urged McCombs to keep Kevin in custody at least until he turned 21 and then put him in an intense rehabilitative program so that he could get on with his young life. He noted that Kevin would be unlikely to receive any significant rehabilitative treatment in an adult prison, but he could in a youth custody center. In an adult prison, Kevin would be exposed to hardened criminals as his only peer group. He wouldn't get any better there, he'd get worse. Kevin's mental illness, Nuttall said, was the root of the problem: "He is not a bad person. He is a sick person."

* * *

Two weeks later, McCombs was ready to pass sentence. It was September 29, 2006. Joanne was there with her sister, Wendy Eberhardt. Ralston didn't show. Kevin Madden Sr. did. Tim Ferriman Sr. was also there.

When summing up what he called a "horrific" crime, McCombs spoke of where the boys stood on that day, almost three years after Johnathon died. He first talked about Tim. "I found his apology to be sincere and his remorse to be genuine." McCombs added that Tim was "very fortunate" to be convicted of manslaughter, indicating that he considered a murder conviction to have been just as likely.

And he also admitted that Tim had made "major strides" at Syl Apps, indicating that, if he played his cards right, he could rejoin society, this time in a better way. But he warned Tim that he wasn't completely sold on him. He added: "There is credible psychiatric evidence before me that if untreated, Mr. Ferriman poses at least a moderate threat" to the public.

Then he turned his attention to Kevin. He called him an "unremorseful, diagnosed psychopath," one who "continues to blame his mother" for all his problems. McCombs said that Kevin "has repeatedly stated that he does not love anyone, nor ever felt love from anyone. He has stated he doesn't know what emotions feel like." McCombs added that there is "credible evidence that he suffers from a deeply entrenched psychological disorder and psychopathy—and that he remains a danger to the public."

After waiting for that to sink in, McCombs announced: "This is not to say that I regard Kevin Madden as unsalvageable."

But that salvage operation would have to wait. McCombs sentenced Kevin Madden to life imprisonment with no chance at parole for 10 years for the murder of Johnathon Madden. He also sentenced him to 10 years—to be served concurrently—for the attempted murder of Ralston Champagnie. Kevin would serve the next two years at a youth facility before being transferred to an adult medium- or maximum-security prison, depending on his behavior.

Timothy Ferriman received two years less a day plus three years probation for the manslaughter conviction related to the death of Johnathon Madden.

He had sentenced them as adults. Brean, Small, Blatchford and the rest of the media realized they could identify Kevin, Tim and Johnathon in their morning editions. Ashley and Pierre, though, would remain protected.

Joanne could make her website.

Kevin was going away for a very, very long time. Tim wouldn't be coming home for a while.

For the first time since Wark interviewed him the day after he killed his brother, Kevin Madden was seen to be crying.

* * *

Outside the courthouse, Brean caught up with Tim Ferriman Sr., who was clearly upset at the outcome of the sentencing. "I expected I'd be taking him home today," he said.

He also confided in the young reporter that since his son's name was going to be public information, he wasn't looking forward to all the explaining he was going to have to do. People had already been talking to him about the case—not realizing "Vampire Boy" was his son—and there were all kinds of untrue rumors circulating about the boys. But at least now he could try to set the record straight.

One of the things he wanted to make clear was that Tim never would have been involved with anything like this if it wasn't for Ashley. "He was influenced by a coquette," he said. "And it's not the first time he's been influenced by a girl. He was naive. I've done it many times myself, fallen for a pretty face."

And Tim's father lashed out at Ashley for her role in the events. "She's very smart for what she did. She was very wise to do it. But I wonder how much participation Tim would have had if she hadn't kept saying, 'Good job, good job.'"

CHAPTER 9

# another year older

With a little more than a year left in Syl Apps on his sentence, Tim Ferriman's long-awaited appeal finally came before a tribunal in October 2007. But by that time, "Vampire Boy" was clearly less of a draw than he had been in the past.

A few minutes before the appeal was to be heard, there was nobody with me in the Osgoode Hall courtroom except a few lawyers—including Dennis Lenzin—before the judges arrived. They were all milling around the courtroom, chatting about various things. I heard one of them say to another: "He's just a total fucking loser." I can't be sure he was talking about Tim, but I wouldn't be all that surprised. The young man whose future was in question didn't show.

Soon we were joined by Peter Small, veteran court reporter for *The Toronto Star*. Peter's a great guy with awesome connections and we started talking about the case and all the people we both knew in local media, police and the justice system.

Just before the proceedings were about to begin, Joanne Champagnie walked in with two associates. One had an ID card hanging from her belt and appeared to be an officer of the court. The other was a family member who had been part of the process from the start. All of the lawyers acknowledged Joanne's entrance with a nod, wave or at least deferential silence. She walked in slowly and deliberately, as though she was having a great deal of trouble getting to her seat. She leaned on her companions for support and occasionally reached for the wall to steady herself. No one spoke until she was seated.

A few minutes after the proceedings actually began, the door opened again and Ashley walked in with one of her friends. She was wearing a tasteful dress and little makeup. She's still pretty, but she has more of a hard, cynical look about her than she used to. She looks a touch older than her 18 years, but no older than a typical college undergrad. Her entry and heavy steps brought the proceedings to a halt. Once she sat—beside Joanne but without acknowledging her—with a loud, seemingly exasperated sigh, the appeal began in earnest.

Tim's lawyer, David Harris, presented a multi-pronged case. He said that Tim had turned his life around at Syl Apps. He'd applied himself and earned a high school diploma—something he was not headed for before the murder.

He also pointed out that Tim had received a harsher sentence than many other people his age who had been convicted of manslaughter.

The judges acknowledged his points with little argument, although one of them pointed out that his academic success at Syl Apps might be an indication that the facility was actually the best place for him—at least for now.

Then Harris stepped into a minefield. He told the judges that he thought Justice David McCombs had erred in his judgment because he had not given equal weight to both expert psychiatric witnesses. He pointed out that Dominique Bourget, the psychiatrist who examined the boys at Royal Ottawa Hospital, and Ian Swayze, the doctor who examined them at Toronto's Center for Addiction and Mental Health after their convictions, had very divergent opinions as to what motivated the killing, and that McCombs had ignored Bourget and accepted Swayze's opinion as gospel.

My experience in courts has shown me that judges really, really don't like it when a lawyer attacks the opinion of one of their own. And nothing that happened that day changed my perspective. The three judges of the tribunal took Harris to task. Taking turns, they lectured him on the rights of a judge and pointed out repeatedly that McCombs had the power to determine the weight he would give the testimony of any witness. If he felt that Swayze had hit the bull's-eye while Bourget had missed the board entirely, it was entirely within his rights to do so. Their arguments on this point took so long and were so thorough, it seemed like they were scolding Harris by the time they finished.

Since Harris had nothing more to say, the judges decided to confer in their chambers. They left for a few minutes and the courtroom once again became animated with conversations between the lawyers and Peter and me. Ashley and her companion stamped out of the courtroom, as if disappointed that Tim wasn't there.

The judges returned after about ten minutes. They took a few moments to thank Harris for his presentation and to point out his long record of thoughtful and professional arguments before the court. Then they told the Crown—a meticulous-looking young man—that they would not need to hear from him today. The defense simply had no case and, if anything, the young man seemed to have been benefiting from his time in custody. Tim Ferriman would be required to serve the rest of his sentence as charged.

After the hearing, Peter and I did our best to grab some of the principals for comments. I bet wrong. While he spoke with Harris, I hopped on an elevator with one of the attorneys from the original two trials and told him who I was and that I was writing a book about the case. He sighed and told me: "I don't speak to the media." Then he paused and added: "Dr. Phil called and I turned him down . . . so what makes you think I'll talk to you?" I didn't have time to see if I could get anything else from him, so I cut my losses and stuck my arm between the closing elevator doors. They popped open and I jumped out to join Peter, who was approaching Joanne. "Just make sure you spell my name right," the lawyer called out as the doors were closing again. "Don't worry," I called back. "It's an easy one."

I ran to join Peter just as he was about to talk to Joanne. Her handlers told us both that she wasn't ready to talk. That was cool. We had to respect that. But I had to finally meet her. By that point we had traded e-mails and spoken on the phone, but had actually never met face to face. I introduced myself—told her she could finally put a face to the many e-mails and phone calls she had gotten from me—and shook her hand.

When our eyes met, I saw something I really wished I hadn't. I saw the sorrow and pain of a parent who had lost both of her sons. I saw the honest truth of tragedy and I could not look away. She tried to smile and said something neither of us remembers.

Then her companions took her to a car and whisked her away. Peter and I walked up the street talking about the case for a few minutes, but soon parted—he had another trial to cover and I had another source to interview.

* * *

While attending Tim's appeal may have thrown her for a loop, by all reports Joanne is doing quite well, given the circumstances. While many of the people I spoke with held Ralston's intractability at least partly responsible for the tragedy that befell the family, she certainly doesn't. They are still married and together.

They no longer live at 90 Dawes, but aren't very far away. The memories aren't far away, either. Detective Sergeant Terry Wark did his best to measure her progress through the Toronto Police Department's victim's services unit. Some time after he was satisfied she was beginning to put it all behind her, he received a call from her. She was complaining that on the walks she and Ralston took around the neighborhood, they occasionally ran into Pierre. It was, she said, very disturbing to see a young man who she believed had helped murder her son and tried to murder her husband. Wark had to sadly tell her there was nothing he could do about it. Pierre had been acquitted. He was a free man. He could walk down the street like anybody else.

Joanne has launched her promised memorial website for Johnathon. It can be seen at http://www.johnathon-madden.memory-of.com. On opening, it plays an mp3 of Bette Midler singing "Wind Beneath My Wings." The front page features a rather serious-looking portrait of Johnathon (his sixth-grade school photo) and a personal tribute written by Joanne. It is followed by an anonymously written poem expressing the hope that the family will be reunited in the afterlife.

The site's second page contains many touching condolences offered by friends, family members and strangers.

What follows is a copy of the eulogy written and delivered by Johnathon's uncle Frank at the funeral. It takes the form of a letter from heaven in which Johnathon assures his family and friends that he is much happier now and that he doesn't want to be remembered for the last few tragic moments of his life, but for the rest of it.

Then there is a photo album that tracks Johnathon's life from infancy to the year of his death. He looks a lot like his mom. Many of the photos are school pictures, but a bunch of them show Johnathon playing, posing or—when he was a toddler—just going about his business. There are 51 photos in the collection and Kevin shows up in none of them. Neither does Ralston or Kevin Madden Sr.

Joanne visits Kevin in prison every once in a while. From all reports, he has not made any significant progress in the psychological treatment he's received in custody and it's unlikely he'll be paroled when he becomes eligible in 2016, when he'll be 29. Nobody I spoke with was of the opinion Kevin would ever be able to shake his anger and violence problems well enough to convince a parole board that he would not re-offend if released. One police officer I spoke with who was familiar with the case and with Kevin told me point blank: "He's not getting out." It has yet to be decided if he will be transferred to a medium or maximum security prison.

Pierre has, as many predicted, shunned the spotlight. He went back to Rosedale Heights and got his diploma a year later than the rest of his class. He still draws a lot and, from what I hear, would like to become a comic-book or animation artist. He continues to get strong support from his parents, who Wark described as "good people" and having "gone through hell for him."

Tim is still in Syl Apps, but should be out before the end of 2008. By all accounts, he seems to be doing well there, responding to his treatments. According to a recently released former inmate I spoke with who knew him, he became much less unpopular among the general population there once he stopped talking in "funny" voices and trying to show off how smart he was all the time. Syl Apps isn't considered a very difficult place for a young man to do time, and Ferriman's stay since his sentencing has been remarkably uneventful.

Ashley graduated from Rosedale Heights and is now enrolled in the arts program at a good university. She's still an avid photographer, but no longer acts. She's toned down her look quite a lot, dressing tastefully and discreetly, pretty much the way any parent would want a daughter her age to look. According to people who know her, she can get some of the old gear out for shows and visits to nightclubs, but even then, she's still rarely outlandish looking.

I spoke with a young man—a drama student at another university—who had befriended her after meeting her at a concert. They communicated for a while, but he stopped, he says, because he found her "too aggressive." He described her as "really good looking," but said he wasn't sure she was "worth the trouble" to continue getting to know.

One former friend of hers from Rosedale Heights told me Ashley had a website where she sold nude photos of herself. I was not surprised when the story turned out to be false.

Heather continues to be Ashley's friend, while Lindsay does not. A person very close to the case described Heather as "having her head screwed on right." He maintains that she's "a good kid with a good family; she'll be alright no matter what she chooses to do." When I asked the same person about Lindsay, he laughed and asked "you mean the little shit? That's what we all called her at the trial." He smiled and told me: "She's in for a surprise when she grows up; she'll find out that most people are not as easy to push around as parents and teachers—good luck to her."

Interestingly, none of the principals seems to have learned much about the Internet since the murder. Pierre and all of the girls have Facebook pages with a surprising amount of personal information on them. Even Tim got into the act. Early in 2007 he advertised on a musicians' site his desire to play bass in a heavy metal band. The ad read like most others in the genre, although he did mention some "special circumstances" that would keep him from joining a band right away. He would, the ad said, explain them to interested parties if they e-mailed him. Still, I could see a lot of heavy metal bands wanting to have a bass player who had done time for manslaughter. If he can play—he couldn't before he went to Syl Apps, but the bass lines in heavy metal are usually pretty remedial—he could become a marketable commodity.

Of course, Ashley's accounts at VampireFreaks and Xanga are long gone, but she still does have a surprising amount of her personal inventory—particularly art photographs—on the Web. Some of them are from around the time of the murder, some from during the trial and some after. There doesn't seem to me to be any progression to the works. The ones from 2007 could just as easily be in the 2003 album. If Johnathon's murder had any effect on her, it didn't show up in her work.

Fearing Ashley's works were perhaps too subtle for me, that maybe I'd missed the point, I showed her photos to an accomplished artist I know well, and she said that they were "technically sound" but the subject matter—homeless people, urban architecture—and its treatment were "typically undergrad" and far from deep. Ashley also had a number of self-portraits on one site (she's since removed them, but they are easy to find for anyone who knows how to handle a search engine cache), which show a distinctly narcissistic bent. One in particular, a loving study of her own legs and buttocks, seems less an artistic effort than an ode to self-edification.

She has turned out pretty much as any close observer of the case may have predicted. She's shaken off the past and recreated herself as a slightly different person. She still has an artistic bent and a healthy sense of self, but has packaged it all into a person who is much more appealing to the public at large. No longer does she claim on the Internet to "bite for blood"; now she parties like any other college student. Gone are the black clothes, thick eyeliner and dour attitude, replaced by tasteful colors, sensible looks and an upbeat personality. If, as many people said during the trial, there were two Ashleys—the calm, endearing witness and the secretive, name-calling perjurer who stalked the Internet proclaiming her love of blood and vampirism—only one seems to have survived.

At least, as far as I know. See, Ashley made a rookie's mistake when she made all those postings Joe Brean discovered back in 2003—she used her real e-mail address when she signed up. Of course, she could now be posting anything she wants over the Internet under an assumed name. But nothing posted to the Internet is ever really untraceable (or truly deletable) and a diligent search of postings from her IP address could yield some surprises.

The other kids largely fell into predictable paths as well. Few who knew Kevin before the murder would be all that surprised to learn that he ended up in prison. He was a big, dumb kid who had a problem following rules and had a sense of entitlement. That he's not responding to treatment in any significant way is no shocker, either. There is simply no tried-and-true remedy for what he has. Whether being behind bars will ever help him is debatable, but it has certainly been safer for the people outside. While the psychiatrists may differ as to exactly what disorder he suffers from, they agree that he is prone to fits of anger during which he is capable of exceptional violence. His continued incarceration is an excellent example for the argument that prisons keep the general population safe by segregating the most violent offenders from the rest of us.

Conversely, Tim could act as a poster child for the rehabilitative qualities of the penal system. Tim, whose many personality problems all seemed to have stemmed from his immaturity and lack of self-confidence, may well have fared better in Syl Apps than he would have outside the facility. He has, by all accounts, reacted well to the discipline (both official and social) imposed by the facility. My sources say that he's lost the smugness, the tantrums, the feeling that he's always right no matter what the situation.

It may well be overly optimistic to think that he will leave the facility a fine, upstanding and well-adjusted member of society, but every source I have agrees that Tim is far more mature and better equipped to be part of the world than he was back in 2003. It's just a shame that it took a multi-year stay in a secure institution to help him.

The only one of the kids who didn't end up where everyone expected was Johnathon himself.

When I was planning this book, I was sure I was going to write a chapter about Johnathon, but it doesn't seem appropriate now. I have spoken with dozens of people—kids, teens, adults, friends, relatives and teachers—who knew Johnathon when he was alive and they all tell basically the same story. He was a typical little boy. He was 12 and liked all the things people expect—or perhaps want—a 12-year-old to like. He liked sports and had a fondness for video games, although not the frightening ones his big brother preferred.

The adults I spoke with who knew him all remember him as flawless. To them, he was an unalloyed, unblemished embodiment of everything that is good and innocent in our world. They tend to use the word "angel" a lot when they describe him. They always point out his love for sports, especially basketball and his hometown Raptors. He also had a fondness for lacrosse and went to go see the Toronto Rock—whose tickets were much cheaper and easier to get than the Raptors'—with Ralston. He also had a fondness for Ralston's cooking, especially traditional Jamaican standards like curried chicken and salt fish. And most of the adults I spoke with mentioned Johnathon's love of classical music, especially the works of Beethoven, which were said to calm him down when he was stressed.

One adult, the mother of a friend of his, said that when Johnathon came over, he acted a little strange sometimes. He was, she said, shy around adults he didn't know—much more so than most kids his age—and would never, ever accept anything offered to him, no matter how small or trivial. She told me she found that strange.

But the children and teens who knew him paint a slightly different, far more realistic picture. He tended to find himself funnier than anyone else did. He had a goofy haircut and he liked to wear gaudy, even ridiculous shirts. Johnathon did all the things you expect—even want—a boy to do. He grossed out girls, chided his classmates, did things behind his teacher's backs and performed risky stunts that would have made his parents cringe if they'd known about them.

But all of the people I spoke with—no matter what their age or their relationship to him—held Johnathon in high regard. He was playful and considered himself something of a class clown. It's hard to find a picture of him when he isn't smiling or at least smirking. He tended to get good, though not great, marks in school. He was just too easily distracted to be a great student. Johnathon had many friends and generally treated them with equal warmth and respect.

In November 2003, at almost exactly 12 1/2 years old, Johnathon was on the cusp of a whole new life. While he enjoyed going to the Santa Claus Parade with his mother only days before he was murdered, he also admitted at about the same time to having a crush on a neighborhood girl and had asked family and friends what kind of restaurant he should take her to for their first date.

Johnathon never went on that date, never had a first kiss. He died before he could enjoy many of other things the rest of us take for granted.

It was a case of being in the wrong place at the wrong time. But what makes his story all the more tragic is that the wrong place was his own home, where a child should be safest. But Johnathon had the bad luck to live in the same house, the same room, as a brother who would torture him for no discernible reason and finally kill him.

Nobody, not even Kevin, disputes that he murdered Johnathon. The courts have decided that Pierre had nothing to do with his death and that Tim only facilitated while Kevin did all the hacking and slashing. And there's nobody around who'll prove them wrong: Kevin continues to accept all blame, Pierre and Tim will admit to nothing more than the tape and eyewitnesses have made absolutely impossible to deny. The only other person present is dead.

The question isn't who did it, but why. The consensus is that Kevin was mentally ill. While there's no doubt that Kevin had deep psychological issues, the doctors I consulted indicated that up to five percent of the entire population share at least some of his problems. If that's what made him kill his brother, it's a true wonder that the murder rate isn't much, much higher than it is.

If you believe Kevin's story, what made him hack his little brother's throat to shreds is the fact that Johnathon said he was going to tell their parents about the mess Kevin and his friends had made. Kevin and Johnathon had probably had bigger conflicts in the past. But this one was different.

Clearly, Kevin knew there was no turning back once Johnathon arrived home. When he took out the bat and started smashing mustard jars, beer bottles and eventually a TV, he must have surmised it would be impossible to live with Ralston any more. They had already gotten to the point where they barely spoke.

The situation at home was bad. Ralston and Joanne had done everything they could to keep the peace in the house—including sending Kevin to mental health professionals and accompanying him to family counseling. If Ralston came home to find his basement entirely trashed and his TV destroyed, Kevin would have been in the most serious trouble of his life. Would he have had to fear for his life? Almost certainly not. But the mind of a teenage boy—especially a psychopathic one—doesn't always work along logical pathways.

Kevin's best friend had just stolen his longtime girlfriend. Ralston had taken the disciplinary reins back, banning him from the family PC. He was failing in school yet again. He had, according to Alex, tried desperately to lose weight and failed at that. For a boy with so little positive stimulus and so limited an intellect, it must have seemed like there was little to live for.

So he came up with a plan. He told his friends he would kill his family, take all of their money and credit cards and live off them until the funds ran out or the cops came. After that he (or they, as he tried to recruit Pierre and Tim) would move to another house, kill its inhabitants, use their cash and credit cards to survive and repeat as necessary.

It may seem ridiculous, but the life plans of many 16-year-old boys are ridiculous. I know mine were. When compared to the more probable future facing Kevin, the guy with the lowest marks and the most behavioral problems in a hard-luck vocational school, the long shot may have appeared the better bet.

* * *

I'm sitting across from Joseph Brean at a pub we're both familiar with. I've been interviewing him for a couple of hours, furiously writing down everything he says. He's a hell of a storyteller and his attention to detail is outstanding.

I have to wrap it up to go get my kids from an after-school program, so I'm getting his views on how the trial fits into a social and historical context. One of the reasons the trial was important, he says, is that there won't be another one like it. Witnesses won't be able to hide behind the anonymity of the Internet anymore.

I have to respectfully disagree. Of course, that day will come, just not right away.

The only reason Ashley got caught in perjury—a crime almost universally acknowledged she committed but was not charged for—was that Brean was curious about how she came up with her e-mail address. By the time he tracked down her all-too-revealing blogs, the jury was already deliberating. And, from my sources, ready to find all three boys guilty.

And even after Brean's front-page story was published, few people involved with the trial read it, and many of them failed to see its significance.

What if Brean hadn't done his search? What if Ashley hadn't blogged under the same name she used as her e-mail address? What if Christie Blatchford hadn't handed David McCaskill Brean's story to see what he thought of his "Bigasskill" nickname? What if he hadn't read it? What if justice David Watt hadn't taken it seriously?

Although Brean's discovery had brought attention to what witnesses are doing online, too many things happened just the right way to expect it to happen consistently from now on.

Brean's just got too much faith in the ability and desire of people—especially those of the age group that run our courts—in power to understand the intricacies of the Internet.

At the time I interview Brean, I'm working for a large daily newspaper. On its editorial staff, there are two distinct groups—the lifers and the kids. The lifers, baby boomers and older, almost universally showed disdain for the Internet. They either found the concept of navigating it too complicated or considered it nothing more than a bad neighborhood full of hucksters and charlatans bent on giving them bad information and trying to get their credit card numbers. Sure they can access online e-mail servers and maybe make a hotel reservation, but they generally fear and distrust the Net. They will gladly use CNN's television broadcasts as a reliable source, but won't touch anything gleaned from cnn.com. And when their old-school research techniques don't pan out (as often happens), they usually hand their work off to one of the kids—who invariably goes to the Net.

The blindness is not limited to journalists. In a speech during a debate on network neutrality, U.S. Senator Ted Stevens (a Republican from Alaska) famously referred to the Internet as "a series of tubes" in 2004, demonstrating a profound ignorance of a medium he had a big role in controlling.

A far more frightening display occurred in May 2007—well after the Johnathon decision—in Britain. Justice Peter Openshaw was hearing a trial about whether Islamic fundamentalists who posted threatening messages on an online forum had violated anti-terrorist laws. During one witness's testimony, Openshaw interrupted and said, "The trouble is I don't understand the language; I don't really understand what a website is."

Aghast, prosecutor Mark Ellison took a few minutes to explain to the 59-year-old judge what "websites" and "forums" were. Later in the case, Openshaw said "I haven't quite grasped the concepts" of the Web and when Ellison introduced a computer expert as a witness, Openshaw asked him, "Will you ask him to keep it simple?"

The trial made "news of the weird" columns in papers around the world, but caused little uproar. Not only was Openshaw not removed from the case, but one of the key defendants changed his plea to guilty.

In the first Johnathon trial, the Internet was barely mentioned before it caused a mistrial. McCaskill did ask Ashley about her "Biteforblood" e-mail address, but when she told him it was the name of a band, he accepted her answer without question. He didn't have a choice, because he didn't have any way to challenge her word.

After Brean broke his story, Lenzin told the judge that he had conducted a Yahoo search of Ashley's name, but it revealed to him nothing of importance.

Who knows how much crucial evidence in this case—and countless others—was missed because the people in charge of finding the truth don't know where or how to look for it?

* * *

While many parents will claim they monitor their children's Internet activities closely—Ashley's said they did—it's not all that realistic an assertion. Younger people just understand the Net better and are quicker to adapt when they have to. They have developed acronyms like CD9 (code 9, parents are around), KPC (keeping parents clueless) and POS (parent reading over my shoulder) to prevent their parents from knowing what they are doing. It's closer to the truth to say that parents have no clue what their children are seeing and posting online.

This lack of parental or official oversight has turned much of the Net into a sort of *Lord of the Flies* scenario where young people largely rule themselves. Want to see the effects? Get an account on VampireFreaks.com and check out some of the profiles closed to non-members.

What all the young people involved in this case had in common other than the Internet is a strong sense of entitlement.

It became very obvious in the second trial when Lindsay had a run-in with Hank Goody. She and some of the other girls started listening to their iPods in court when the subject matter didn't interest them. At first, everybody in the court ignored it—pretended it wasn't happening—but when Lindsay started singing along, it was just too much. A number of court officers told her to stop. She refused. Eventually, Goody himself told her to stop. She refused again. Goody then told her that if she didn't lose the iPod, she would be banned from the courtroom. Lindsay exploded, threw something of a tantrum and told Goody that he couldn't ban her from the courtroom. She was a citizen and she had a right to be there. Goody banned her from the courtroom.

They all had that same sense of entitlement. Kevin clearly felt it was his right to torture and then kill his younger brother because the world had not been fair to him. Tim considered himself entitled to Ashley's affections despite her not considering him worthy of them. Even Gabriel—though bitter, lonely and clearly stupid—thought he was in a position to mentor Kevin and to tell the whole world what it was doing wrong. Sadly and predictably, he exorcised his own inadequacies at the expense of those who had different ancestors than he did.

And it wasn't just the disadvantaged, the losers. Ashley had it all. She was beautiful, rich, intelligent, talented and charismatic. And Ashley felt that she—apparently—was perfectly within her rights to lie under oath as a star witness in a brutal murder case in order to get the use diet she wanted.

That all-pervading sense of doing what's right for oneself no matter the situation that tied them all together isn't a psychological malady or disorder, it's adolescence.

But when this particular group of adolescents—admittedly more malevolent and less disciplined than most—coalesced, it ignited the fuse on a series of events that culminated in the horrific death of Johnathon Madden.

It kind of makes you wonder who's to blame. Obviously Kevin killed his little brother, but Tim and Pierre did encourage his outrageously destructive behavior that day. Ashley praised his murderous plan with her accepting phrase "good job." Joanne and Ralston embittered Kevin by lavishing affection on his brother and showing little but scorn for him. Even if you don't believe Ralston abused Kevin, he did keep pushing his buttons and punishing him in a way that only made his bubbling anger even worse. Kevin's best friend Alex and his girlfriend Katie betrayed him not just by hooking up, but by flaunting it in his face.

Gabriel amplified and helped focus Kevin's hatreds, and lectured him on the "beauty of death." Kevin's teachers, principals and counselors decided to pass him onto one another like the proverbial hot potato, rather than take the responsibility to deal with his problems or remove him from their system. The healthcare professionals who saw him before the murder failed to recognize how disturbed and potentially violent he really was, or if they did, they failed to do anything about it.

While I sincerely doubt too many of them will share the blame, I'm sure at least some of them will share the guilt.

* * *

When students went back to class at Rosedale Heights School of the Arts after the holiday break in January 2008, grief cousellors went with them. The students there were grieving over another murder, one that hit even closer to home than Johnathon's.

Stefanie Rengel was a cute, vivacious 14-year-old in ninth grade. She was well known for her intelligence, good marks in school and kindness. She dyed her hair dark and streaky, wore black a lot and had a ring in her nose, but she was no Goth. "More like a hippie chick," a friend of hers told me, quick to point out that there was nothing "dark about her soul," that she was upbeat, caring and optimistic.

Although the case is still before the courts, her friends, neighbors and police tell a remarkably consistent story. On the afternoon of January 1, Stefanie was at home relaxing when she answered the door. The caller was Dave (not his real name), her ex-boyfriend. Stefanie and Dave had gone out together earlier that year and he was the first guy she'd ever really called her boyfriend. But there were some problems.

Dave was very insecure. He carried quite a bit of weight—always had—and was very sensitive about it. For various reasons, he was not popular with kids his own age (he was 17), so he tended to hang out with those much younger than he was. At first, Stefanie was impressed that an older guy would be so interested in her, but soon grew tired of his emotional immaturity and told him their relationship was over.

When he showed up at her door on New Year's Day, my sources say, she was surprised to see him. But because he told her he had something important to talk about, she agreed to go for a walk with him.

Not far from home, police allege, Dave stabbed Stefanie repeatedly in the abdomen, then left her desperately clinging to life in a snowbank.

A friend of hers, who may have witnessed the attack, called 911. Because of the darkness, snow and the fact that Stefanie was still ambulatory for some time after the stabbing, it took hours to find her. She was eventually discovered near the intersection of Northdale Boulevard and Hollinger Road, not far from her house, by what newspapers described as "an off-duty cop." He then called an ambulance, and she was rushed to a nearby hospital and pronounced dead on arrival.

Ordinarily, the details of a case like this would never be released to the media—after all, the victim was 14 and the alleged murderer 17. But there were some extenuating circumstances at play in this one.

Perhaps the most important one came as a result of Stefanie's popularity and her friends' familiarity with the Internet. Within hours of her death, postings all over the Internet, mainly Facebook, not only announced her death, but named the suspect and accused a conspirator, among other details. The posts, literally hundreds of them, alleged that Dave's new girlfriend, Diana (not her real name), had pressured him to kill Stefanie because she was suspicious that he still loved her and because seeing Stefanie every day at school made her jealous. Both David and Diana were arrested and charged with first-degree murder.

Another mitigating circumstance was that her parents asked the court to make some details of the case public, including Stefanie's name. While it's not uncommon for parents to make such a request, it's not often granted. But the court had reason to believe that Stefanie's parents knew what they were doing—they were both cops. In fact, not only were both of her biological parents cops, but so were both of the people they married after they split up. Stefanie lived with her mother and stepfather, and they were no strangers to homicide. Her mother, Patricia Hung, became known to many in Toronto in July 2004 when she heroically tried to save the life of four-year-old Scarlett Chen, who was murdered by her mother. Stefanie's stepfather was James Hung, who coincidentally had led the ETF assaults on 90 Dawes and Tim Ferriman's place. It was later revealed that her stepfather was the off-duty officer who found her near-lifeless body, about three blocks from where Kevin Madden and Pierre were arrested for Johnathon's murder.

In preliminary hearings, Diana's defense strategy has been to maintain that since she wasn't present at the attack, she is not guilty of the murder. Her lawyer, Marshall Sack, told Justice David McCombs that she is a "straight-A" student and a "very bright young lady." He answered the charge that she pressured David into killing Stefanie by maintaining that his client was misinterpreted by a disturbed and overzealous young man. "My client is alleged to have indicated at some point in time that she wanted the deceased not to be alive. Beyond that, I see nothing, and that's not first-degree murder," he said. "All of us, all of us in our daily lives express feelings, but very few of us know something's going to happen. There's no indication in any of the material that my client, for want of a better expression, put this young man up to this."

When he requested bail for her, Sack pointed out that Diana had been compelled to spend her 16th birthday at Syl Apps. Crown Attorney countered that argument by saying: "Parents would prefer their children not go there [Syl Apps] . . . but parents would also prefer their children would not be in the grave."

She was denied bail.

* * *

The Rengel case is pertinent to the Johnathon murder not because of its many similarities and co-incidences, but because of its differences.

Just 25 months earlier, when Kevin, Tim and Pierre went to trial, what could be gathered from the Internet was considered largely inconsequential to a murder case. Only when it was introduced as inarguably important evidence, did anyone involved give it any credence—and even then, many were still reluctant.

That was 2005; things are different in 2008. Soon after Stefanie's body was found, hundreds of people were discussing the case online. Almost all of them posted evidence that was contrary to the *Youth Criminal Justice Act* and many complained about the existence of the Act itself. Not only did the posters go unpunished for breaking the law, they accomplished something they wanted—many details of the case were made public.

Justice McCombs has clearly learned to respect the power of the Internet after his experience with the first Johnathon trial. An argument could be made that his hand was forced by the Internet again. What good would it do to prevent the mainstream media from publishing the details of the case when hundreds of bloggers and other individuals are already doing so? It's not realistic to think that all of them could be tracked down through their ISPs. It's possible, but it would cost millions, take a long time and, most likely, yield little of value in court. While nothing is ever truly anonymous online, the chances of getting punished for what you say or do are very slim, and that degree of unaccountability is made exponentially more sure if you are part of a large group.

Just as the Internet played a key role in determining the outcome of the Johnathon case, so it has already changed the Rengel case and perhaps endangered a law many disagree with. This successful public defiance of an unpopular law through the power of the Internet won't go unnoticed among politicians, the judiciary and others who set policy. While it would take more than the found blogs of a star witness or the defiant postings of a few hundred grief-striken Torontonians to change public policy, what these cases show is that the Internet is a powerful force.

The era in which the Internet and other forms of electronic communication are commonplace and vital is clearly well underway. But the era in which those forms of communication are recognized as being of the same value as more traditional media is just dawning. Those who fail to acknowledge it—as many did in the Johnathon case—do so at their own peril.

# index


## A

Adrianople, Battle of, 40
Aftab, Parry, 57
aggressiveness/aggressive (symptom, APD), 80, 81, 82, 87
Alans, emperor, 40
Alaric, king of Visigoths, 40
Alex (pseud.), 136, 161, 165
aliases, 80
*Alien* (film), 52
alienation, 36, 53, 54, 116
Alien Sex Fiend (band), 51
*American History X* (film), 137
*American Journal of Psychiatry*, 80
animals, cruelty to, 44, 81
Antisocial Personality Disorder (APD), 79
  symptoms, 80.
  (*See also* psychopaths; sociopaths)
Armstrong, Robert, 102, 103
Ashley (pseud.), 96, 97, 112, 113, 157
  and Internet, 128, 140, 157, 158, 163
  –blogs, 129–133, 162
  and mistrial, 134, 163
  at appeal, 152, 154
  at trial, 130, 131
  cross-examination of, 113–115
  follow-up on, 15
  narcissism, 158
  perception by jury, 113, 115, 131, 133, 134
  perjury, 158, 162, 164
  physical appearance, 2, 96, 112, 115, 153, 158
  relationship with Heather, 115
  relationship with Joseph Brean, 130–32
  relationship with parents, 2, 9, 130
  relationship with Tim Ferriman, 2, 3, 4, 114, 115
  role of, 122–23
  *69 call, 10, 11
  tapes, xi, xii, 11, 13–18, 23, 24, 30, 96, 97, 115
*Associated Press*, 56
attempted murder, 24, 27, 113, 123, 125, 142, 150
Attention Deficit/Hyperactivity Disorder (ADHD), 74, 77, 80
  study of, 75, 76
  symptoms, 75
  treatment of, 78, 79

## B

Badham, John, 51
bail, 140, 167
Balderston, John, 48, 49
Balkans, 40
Ball, Jerry, 29
Banshees (band), 51
Barrett, Paul, M., 84
Batcave (nightclub), 51
batcavers, 52
Bauhaus (band), 51
"Bela Lugosi's Dead" (song), 51
Benótto, Mary Lou, 140
Berelman, Jethro (Jet), 55, 57

Besarab, king of Turks, 44
betting, off-track, 16
Black, Conrad, 127
Blatchford, Christie, 126, 127, 131, 132, 133, 151, 162
blogs, 129–134, 162. *See also* internet
blood, beliefs about, 61–62
Bodo, Atilla, 100, 101
Bogle, Ron, 100, 101
Boone, Carole Ann, 90
Boston Strangler. *See* DeSalvo, Albert
Bourget, Dominique, 116, 117, 118, 124, 145, 153
Bowie, David, 52
boyars (aristocratic tribe), 43, 44
Bradshaw, Erin, 29
Brean, Joseph, 126, 130, 132, 133, 134, 135, 136, 151, 158, 161, 162, 163
  relationship with Ashley, 127–129
*British Medical Journal*, 53
*Buffy the Vampire Slayer* (TV), 36
Bundy, Ted, 82, 86–91
Byzanitium, *39*

C

Campbell, Caryn, 89
Carilion Saint Abans Behavioral Health Center (VA), 84
Castle of Ortranto, 76
Centers for Disease Control and Prevention (Atlanta), 62
Centre for Addiction and Mental Health (Toronto), 38, 72, 92, 144, 153
Centre of Forensic Sciences (Toronto), 104
Champagnie, Joanne, 6, 20, 27, 39, 99, 143, 152, 161
  and discipline, 105
  and house fire, 67
  and media, 154
  and memorial website, 148, 151, 155
  and prison visits, 156
  at appeal, 152
  at sentencing, 150
  attempted suicide of, 105
  reaction to testimony, 104, 109, 112, 121, 144
  reaction to verdict, 142
  relationship with husband, 6, 105, 155
  relationship with sons, 32, 104, 108, 121, 143, 144, 165
  victim impact statement, 146–147
Champagnie, Ralston
  and anger, 6, 18, 20, 21
  and confrontation, 21, 22
  and house fire, 66
  and police, 99
  cross-examination of 107
  description of, 20
  employment, 7, 10, 16
  escape attempt, 22, 23
  guilt, sense of, 148
  relationship with wife, 6, 105, 155
  relationship with stepsons, 6, 10, 20, 21, 22, 23, 105, 106, 108, 148, 165
  victim impact statement, 148
  views on Toronto, 68
Chaney, Lon, 49
*Charmed* (TV), 36
Charron, Stephan, 99

Chess, Stella, 76–78
Children's Aid Society of Toronto, 107
Cho, Seung-Hui, 82–85. *See also* Virginia Tech University
Ciba, 78
Ciba-Geigy, 78
Citytv, 68
Clark, Lynn Schofield, 36
CNN, 162
Collective Soul (band), 83
Columbine High School (CO)
  massacre at, xi, 54, 55
communications. *See* e-mail; tapes; internet
conformity, 35, 37, 41, 52, 54, 58, 137
Constantinople, 39
Cook, William, 101
Cooper, Alice, 51
Coroner's Office of Ontario, 112
Correctional Service of Canada (CSC), 93
Courtenay, William, 49
Crane, Hart, 48
Crouse, Roy, 84

D
Da Ronch, Carol, 88
Dacia (modern Romania), 39
Dahlia (pseud.)
  and Goths, 35
  description of, 32–33
  relationship with Tim Ferriman, 33, 34
Dahmer, Jeffrey, 81
Danube River, 39
Dave (pseud.). *See* Rengel, Stefanie
David (pseud.), 69
  relationship with Madden, Keven, 70, 71
Dawson College (Montreal), 55
Dead Can Dance (band), 51
Deane, Harry, 47, 48
death-metal (music style), 4
*Deathtrap Dungeon* (video game), 7
Deneuve, Catherine, 52
Dennis, John, 140, 149
dentistry, forensic, 112
DeSalvo, Albert ("Boston Strangler"), 81
Diana (pseud.), 166, 167
Dicks, Christopher, 110, 111
DNA, 111
Don Valley (Toronto), 4, 14, 118, 140, 142
*Dracula*
  and copyright, 46, 47, 50, 51
  films, 49, 50, 51
  novel, 42
  plays, 48, 49, 50
DSMMD *(Diagnostic and Statistical Manual of Mental Disorders)*, 80
*Dungeons & Dragons* (video game), 7

E
e-mail, 3, 31, 32, 33, 34, 96, 128, 129, 136, 137, 143, 163
empathy, 80, 145
*Eat My Pussy* (video), 7
Eberhardt, Wendy, 150
*Edmonton Journal*, 59
Ellison, Mark, 163
Emergency Task Force, (Toronto Police Service), 24, 26, 99, 101, 167
entitlement, sense of, 164, 165
Evans, Daniel, Jack, 87

existentialism, 51, 79, 80. *See also* Sartre, Jean-Paul

## F

Facebook (Internet), 157, 166
*Fallen Angel* (Langton), 32
fashion. *See* Goths; New Romantics; Modern Primitive; Punk
Faulkner, William, 48
Ferriman, Tim
  and Dahlia, 33, 34
  and Goth movement, 3, 38
  and mother, 2, 118
  and vampirism, 4, 34, 60, 62, 65, 114, 151
  appeal of, 152, 153, 154
  arrest of, 27
  as "Vampire Boy", 151, 152
  confession of, 26
  cross-examination of, 120
  defense strategy, 114
  demeanor at trial, 111, 112, 143
  description of, 1, 2, 3, 4, 5
  follow-up on, 156, 157
  media coverage of, 95
  reaction to verdict, 142, 143
  rehabilitation of, 158, 159
  relationship with Ashley, 1, 2, 3, 4, 120, 151, 164
  relationship with peers, 3
  remorse of, 148, 150, 155
  role of, 18, 19, 25, 160, 165
  sentence, 150, 153
  trial of, 95, 96
Ferriman, Tim, Sr., 26, 150, 151
fetish, 118
54 Division (Toronto Police Service), 27
fire, 66–68, 133, 138–39. *See also* Toronto Fire Services
first-degree murder, 30, 102, 122, 125, 142, 166, 167
Fischer, Eric, 58
Flynn, Errol, 50
Forensic Identification Service (Toronto Police Service), 102, 103
forensics, physical, 103, 104
*Frankenstein* (play), 48
*From Angels to Aliens: Teenagers, the Media and the Supernatural* (Clark), 36

## G

Gable, Clark, 50
Gacy, John Wayne, 81
games (video), 6, 7, 17, 105, 116, 117, 119, 159. *See also* specific titles.
Gerard, Robert, 104
Gill, Kimveer ("Angel of Death,") 55–57. *See also* Dawson College
Giovanni, Nikki, 83, 85
*Globe and Mail, 126, 127*
Goody, Hank, 96, 98, 100, 104–6, 110–12, 117, 119, 124, 139, 148, 149, 164
Google (Internet), 129, 132, 133
gothic
  architectural style, 41
  film style, 47
  horror, 51
  literary style, 41, 42
goth metal (music style), 56, 57
Goths, 2, 3, 35, 37, 38, 39, 41, 52–58, 60, 61, 63, 129, 138. *See also* batcavers; Ostrogoths; Visigoths
Gray, Glenn, 17, 18, 23, 24, 26, 27, 28, 32, 97
Green, Anne-Marie, 67, 68

Green River Killer, 91
Greenwood Raceway, 16
Grewal, Karan, 82, 83
guilt, lacking sense of (symptom, APD), 80
grundge (music style), 56

## H

Habsburg, Dominic von, 45
Hageman, Cecilia, 111
Hammer Films, 50
handcuffs, 8, 88, 89
Hare, Robert, 86, 92, 93, 94
Harker, John, 45, 46
Harper Hall (Virginia Tech University), 82, 87
Harris, David, 149, 153, 154
Harris, Eric, 55
Haynes, Chris, 29
hearing, preliminary, 111, 140
Heather (pseud.), 10, 11, 12, 15, 16, 28, 97, 157
Hemingway, Ernest, 48
heritage, Judeo-Christian, 36
*High Risk: Children Without a Conscience* (Magid), 92
Hippocrates, of Cos II, 74, 75
Honorious, emperor, 40
*Horror of Dracula* (film), 50
*How to Help Your Child Get the Most Out of School* (Chess), 77
*Hunchback of Notre Dame* (film), 49
Hung, James, 21, 99, 100, 101, 167
Hung, Patricia, 167
Hungary, 42, 43, 48
*Hunger, The*
  novel (Streiber), 52
  film, 52
Huns (tribe), 39, 40
Huntley, Richard, 48
Hunyadi, John, 43
hyperactivity, 76, 77
  treatment of, 78
  (*See also* Attention Deficit/Hyperactivity Disorder, Ritalin)

## I

impulsivity (symptom, APD), 7, 80
indifference (symptom, APD), 80
industrial (music style), 56
insanity, as defense, 113, 122
Intermittent Explosive Disorder, 118, 122, 124, 141, 143
Internet, 3, 32, 38, 54–58, 126, 128, 129, 133, 135, 136, 157, 158, 162–64, 166, 168.
*Interview With the Vampire* (Rice), 52
investigative unit (Toronto Police Service), 17
irritability (symptom, APD), 80
irresponsibility (symptom, APD), 80

## J

Jackpot (nickname) 127
Jamal (pseud.), 12, 98
Jeffrey, 12, 97, 98
*Jerry Springer* (TV), 35
Jet (Berelman, Jethro), 55, 57
jury
  charge to, 125
  decision of, 142

## K

Katie, 104, 105, 121, 136, 137, 165
Kew Beach (Toronto), 1

Kidman, Nicole, 86
King's College Hospital (London, England), 75
Klebold, Dylan, 55
K-Mart, 60
*Know Your Child* (Chess), 77
Koch, Andy, 83

## L

Lacey (WA), 63
Laemme, Carl, Jr., 49
Lance (Lee, Andrew), 55
lancets, 61
Langella Frank, 50, 51
Leader (SK), 59
Leck, David, 100
Lee, Andrew (Lance), 55
Lee, Christopher, 50, 51
Lenzin, Dennis, 108, 110, 123, 132, 133, 140, 141, 142, 152, 163
Levine, Marie, 145, 146, 149
Lindsay (pseud.), 11, 12, 16, 28, 157, 164
Liveright, Horace, 48
Longobards (tribe), 41
*Love At First Bite* (film), 50
Lugos (Lugoj, Romania), 48
Lugosi, Bela (Blasko, Bela), 48–51

## M

MacDonald, John, 80, 81
Madden, Johnathon
- and Frank (uncle), 155
- and house fire, 67
- death of, 18, 19, 24, 26, 109, 100, 110
- description of, 148, 159, 160
- eulogy for, 155
- injuries suffered by, 28, 109, 110
- innocence of xii, 11, 148
- relationship with father (biological), xi, 6, 116
- relationship with mother, 6, 104, 108, 121, 160, 165
- relationship with stepfather, 105, 106, 108, 148, 165
- relationship with peers, 12, 16, 17, 98, 99, 159, 160
- memorial to, 148, 151, 155

Madden, Kevin
- abuse of, 107, 116, 121
- and bullying, 71
- and discipline, 5, 6, 20, 21
- and house fire, 67, 68
- and Intermittent Explosive Disorder, 118
- and jury, 112, 122
- and media, 29
- and rampage, 8, 11
- appearance of, 5, 68, 158
- arrest of, 29, 31, 158
- as leader, 7
- as psychopath, 72, 145, 146, 150, 161
- attack on Johnathon, 18, 19, 25, 26, 109, 110
- follow-up, 156, 158
- hiding, from police, 23, 25, 28, 29, 120
- insanity, as defense of, 113, 122
- interrogation of, 29, 30
- mental health of, xi, 68, 69, 113, 116, 118, 122, 160, 161
- plan to murder, 9, 14, 15, 18, 19, 22, 23, 29, 32, 124, 125, 142, 161
- relationship with father (biological), xi, 6, 116, 137
- relationship with Gabriel Verventiotis, 136, 137, 138, 139, 164, 165

relationship with mother, 6, 32, 108, 121, 143, 144, 165
relationship with peers, 5, 69, 71, 137
relationship with stepfather, 6, 8, 20, 21, 22, 23, 108, 161
sentencing of, 150, 151
treatment, suggested, 148
trial of 95, 96, 111
truancy of, 5, 6, 10, 21
Madden Kevin Sr., 148, 150, 156.
Magid, Ken, 92
*Malice* (film), 86
Mandel, Michelle, 143
manslaughter, 122, 141, 142, 143, 150, 153, 157
Marcianopolis (Bulgaria), 39
Marilyn Manson (band), 38, 55
*Matrix, The* (film), 98
McCaskill, David, 101, 110, 114, 115, 118, 120, 123, 127, 128, 131, 132, 139, 162, 163
McCombs, David, 140, 142–46, 148–50, 153, 167, 168
McLaren, Malcolm, 53, 54
McKeown, Rick, 103, 104
Medicine Hat (Alta), 58, 59
Mehmed II, sultan, 44
MGM, 52
mental health
diagnosing, 80
gender differences, 81
treatment facilities. *See* names
(*See also* sociopath; psychopath)
Mercer, Mick, 56
*Mick, The* (magazine), 56
Midler, Bette, 155
Ministry of Community Safety and Correctional Services (Ontario), 104
Mircea (brother, Vlad III), 43
mistrial, 134, 140, 163
Modern Primitives (fashion), 52
Morris, Chester, 49
MSN Messenger, 3, 5, 31, 33, 34, 115, 119. *See also* internet
MuchMusic (TV network), 37, 38
Multi-Health Systems, 93
Muni, Paul, 49
murder
attempted, 24, 27, 113, 123, 125, 142, 150
first-degree, 30, 102, 122, 125, 142, 166, 167
–compared to manslaughter, 122
manslaughter, 141, 142, 143, 150, 153, 157
murderers, mental health, 80–81. *See also* serial killers
Murnau, Freidrich Wilhelm, 46, 47
Murray, Steve, 132
music, styles of, 51, 56, 57. *See also* punk; post-punk; grundge; rock; goth metal; industrial
MySpace (Internet), 29
mythology, 37

## N

*National Post*, 126, 127, 132, 133, 139
Nazism, xi, 137, 138, 139
narcissism, 81, 158
NBC, 85
neo-classical (architecture), 41
New River Valley Community Services Board (VA), 84
New Romantics (fashion), 52

*New York Longitudinal Study of Child Development* (Chess), 77
North, David, 140
Norton, Edward, 137
*Nosferatu, eine Symphonie des Grauens* (Nosferatu, Symphony of Horror), 46, 47
Nova Roma. *See* Byzantium
Novartis, 78
*Now* (magazine), 55
Nuttall, Robert, 105, 107, 108, 114, 118, 120, 122, 123, 149

O

Oath, Hipprocratic, 71
occult, 4
*Onion, The,* (newspaper) 74
Ontario Centre for Forensic Sciences, 111
Ontario Ministry of Labour, 139
Openshaw, Peter, 163
Osgoode Hall (Toronto), 152
Ostrogoths, 39, 40, 41
Ottoman Empire, 43, 44, 45

P

parade, Santa Claus, 160
paramedics, 25, 26, 100
Parker, Dorothy, 48
Perelman, S.J., 48
perfectionism, pathological, 61
perjury, 131, 133, 134, 158, 162, 164
personality, type-A, 92
*Phantom of the Opera* (film), 49
Pierre (pseud.), 5, 6
  acquittal of, 142, 155, 160
  and bail, 140
  and parents, 96, 156
  arrest of, 29, 102
  at trial, 95, 96, 111, 114
  defense strategy for, 114
  follow-up on, 156
  hiding, from police, 23, 25, 28, 29, 120
  mental health of, 111
  relationship with Madden, Kevin, 6, 7, 8
  role of, 7, 8, 18, 19, 23, 106, 108, 118, 119, 123, 165
  verdict *See* Pierre, acquittal
plan, to kill, 9, 18, 19, 22, 23, 32, 124, 125, 142. *See also* Madden, Kevin
plea bargain, 95
Pollanen, Michael, 108, 109, 110
Poole, Julian, 82
Post-Encephalitic Behavior Disorder, 76
post-punk (music style), 51
Prana-Film GmbH (film production), 47
prisoners' rights
  –comparison to U.S., 27
psychopaths, 72, 86, 87, 145, 146, 149, 150, 161
  causes of, 92, 93
  characteristics of, 72, 73, 81, 82, 91
  compare to sociopath, 82, 83, 91, 92
  treatment of, 93, 94
  (*See also* sociopaths)
publication ban, 95, 148, 151
punk: fashion, 53, 54; music style, 51

Q

"Question Mark Kid". *See* Cho, Seung-Hui

## R

racism, 70, 99, 138, 139
Radu, the Handsome, 44
Rais, Gilles de, 42
rampage, 119
recklessness (symptom, APD), 80
*Red Poppy, The* (play), 48
remorselessness (symptom, APD), 80, 105, 145, 146, 150, 157, 161
Rengel, Stefanie, 165–68
Rice, Anne, 52
Ritalin, 78, 79. *See also* Attention Deficit/Hyperactivity Disorder
rivalry, sibling, 126
River Danube, 39
rock (music style), 56
Roman Empire, 38–40
romanticism, 51
*Romeo and Juliet* (play), xii, 84
Rosedale Heights School of the Arts (Toronto), 2, 5, 7, 10, 11, 14, 156, 157, 166
Rossano, John, 29, 102
Roy, Lucinda, 83
Royal Ontario Hospital (Ottawa), 116, 153
*Runescape* (video game), 17

## S

Sack, Marshall, 167
Salarian Gate, 40
Sanctuary: the Vampire Sex Bar (Toronto), 38, 55
*sanguineus*, 61
Sarah (pseud.), 125
Sarandon, Susan, 52
Sarte, Jean-Paul, 79, 80
satanism, xi, xii, 116, 117
Savage Garden (club, Toronto), 38
Sawyer, Diane, 54
Scott, Ridley, 52
Scott, Tony, 51, 52
Schreck, Max, 46
Sean, 16, 17, 125
  testimony of, 98, 99
sentences
  options for, 143
  passing of, 150
  recommendations for, 148, 149
serial killers. *See also* names
Seto, Michael, 92
Sex Pistols (band), 53
Sherk, Chris, 29, 101, 102
"Shine" (song), 83
Shopsy's, 7, 10, 16
Siouxsie (band), 51
Sisters of Mercy (band), 51
Small, Peter, 126, 132, 133, 142, 151, 152, 154
sociopaths, 81, 82, 83, 86, 91, 92. *See also* psychopaths
Specimen (band), 51
*spiritus*, 61
Sprucedale Youth Centre (Simcoe), 143, 145, 146
Song, Vivian, 126
Starbucks, 38
statements
  on sentencing, 148
  victim impact, 146, 147, 148
Stein, Steven, 92
Steinke, Jeremy Allen, 59
stepfather. *See* Champagnie, Ralston
Stevens, Ted, 163
Stilicho, Flavius general, 40
Still, George Frederic, 75, 76, 77

Still's Disease, 75
Stoker, Bram, 42, 44. *See also* *Dracula*
Stoker, Florence, 47, 50
Streiber, William, 52
Sunnybrook Hospital (Toronto), 101
Suplee, Ethan, 137
Swayze, Ian, 144, 146, 149, 153
Syl Apps, 31
Syl Apps Youth and Secure Treatment Centre (Oakville), 31, 148, 149, 150, 152, 156, 158, 167

T

tapes, xi, xii, 11, 13–18, 23, 24, 30, 96, 97, 115
Taylor Creek (Toronto), 21, 25, 28, 120
Tenhouse, Anna, 110, 111, 144, 145
Tepes, Vllad, king. *See* Vlad, the Impaler
*Texas Chainsaw Massacre* (film), 47
The Cure (band), 51
Theodosius, emperor, 40
Thomas, Alexander, 76
"Threat to Kill" (MacDonald), 80
threats, death, 121
Toronto Fire Services, 66, 67, 68
Toronto Police Service
  Emergency Task Force, 24, 26, 99, 101, 167
  54 Division, 27
  Forensic Identification Unit, 102, 103
  Victim Services Unit, 155
*Toronto Star*, 126, 127, 142, 152
*Toronto Sun, 143*
*Touched by an Angel* (TV), 36
Transylvania, 42, 43, 44
trauma, childhood, 76
trial
  first trial, xii, 111
  judges *See* names
  lawyers *See* names
  reporting of, 95, 113, 148
  second trial, 140
  testimony at, 97, 98, 99, 107, 118, 127, 128, 130, 131, 134, 141, 148.
  *See also* names of witnesses
  verdict, 142
  witnesses, expert, 118, 124. *See also* names
  (*See also* mistrial, jury)
Trojan Horse, 40
truancy, 3, 5, 6, 10

U

Ummayyads (tribe), 41
Universal Studios, 49
University of British Columbia, 86
University of Washington, 87

V

Valens, emperor, 40
Vampirism, xi, 4, 9, 34, 35, 36, 37, 50, 59, 116, 117, 118, 126, 141
  and *Dracula*, 46
  and media, 60
  and *The Hunger*, 52
  as scam, 64
  –comparison to Goths, 60
  creed of, 64
  legend (myth) of, 35, 36, 42, 62
  motto of, 63

regional differences of, 42
role of blood, 36, 61, 62
websites, pertaining to, 55, 57, 59, 129, 133, 155, 163, 164
Vandals (tribe), 40
Veidt, Conrad, 49
Velvet Underground (club), 38
verdict, 142
Verventiotis, Gabriel, 136, 137, 138, 139, 164, 165
victim services unit (Toronto Police Service), 155
Virginia Tech University, 82
massacre at, 84
Visigoths, 39, 41. *See also* Goths
Vlad, the Impaler, 42, 43

W

Walpole, Horace, 41, 42
"Wind Beneath My Wings" (song), 155
Wallachia (Romania), 43
Wark, Terry, 29, 30, 139, 151, 155, 156
Watt, David, 97, 125, 133, 134, 162
Websites
and vampirism, 55, 57, 59, 129, 133, 155, 163, 164
memorial for Johnathon, 148, 155.
(*See also* internet)
Wildeboer, Paul, 16, 17, 18, 97
Wilson, Sheila, 92
*Wings* (film), 47. *See also* Murnau, Friedrich Wilhelm
Wired Safety, 57. *See also* internet
Wisdom, Olli, 51
Wood, Robert, 112, 123
Woodbine (race track, Toronto), 16
wounds, defensive, 109
Wray, John, 49

Y

Yahoo (internet), 133, 163
*Your Child As a Person* (Chess), 77
Youth Criminal Justice Act (Young Offender's Act), 30, 168

Z

Zoosadism. *See* animals, cruelty to